OECD ECONOMIC SURVEYS

FINLAND

JUNE 1986

ORGANISATION FOR ECONOMIC CO-OPERATION AND DEVELOPMENT

Pursuant to article 1 of the Convention signed in Paris on 14th December, 1960, and which came into force on 30th September, 1961, the Organisation for Economic Co-operation and Development (OECD) shall promote policies designed:

- to achieve the highest sustainable economic growth and employment and a rising standard of living in Member countries, while maintaining financial stability, and thus to contribute to the development of the world economy;
- to contribute to sound economic expansion in Member as well as non-member countries in the process of economic development; and
- to contribute to the expansion of world trade on a multilateral, non-discriminatory basis in accordance with international obligations.

The Signatories of the Convention on the OECD are Austria, Belgium, Canada, Denmark, France, the Federal Republic of Germany, Greece, Iceland, Ireland, Italy, Luxembourg, the Netherlands, Norway, Portugal, Spain, Sweden, Switzerland, Turkey, the United Kingdom and the United States. The following countries acceded subsequently to this Convention (the dates are those on which the instruments of accession were deposited): Japan (28th April, 1964), Finland (28th January, 1969), Australia (7th June, 1971) and New Zealand (29th May, 1973).

The Socialist Federal Republic of Yugoslavia takes part in certain work of the OECD (agreement of 28th October, 1961).

Publié également en français.

CONTENTS

TABLES

DIAGRAMS

BASIC STATISTICS OF FINLAND

THE LAND

Area (1 000 sq. km)	338	Population in major cities, 1983:	
of which:		Helsinki	484 471
Cultivated land	27	Tampere	167 344
Forests	187	Turku	163 002
Lakes	32	Urban population (per cent of total)	60

THE PEOPLE

Total population (1984), thousands	4 894	Manpower by industry in 1984 (per cent of total):	
Per sq. km of land area	15.8	Agriculture and forestry	12
Average (1980-84, per thousand):		Industry and construction	33
Live births	13.5	Commerce	14
Deaths	9.2	Transport and communication	7
Net natural increase	4.2	Services	34
Net increase of population	4.7		

PARLIAMENT AND GOVERNMENT

Composition of Parliament, number of seats (1983):		Government, number of ministers	
Social Democratic Party	57	from:	
National Coalition (Conservatives)	44	Centre Party	5
Centre Party[1]	38	Social Democratic Party	8
Democratic Union (including Communists)	27	Swedish People's Party	2
Swedish People's Party	11	Finnish Rural Party	2
Christian Union	3		
Rural Party	17	Total	17
"Greens"	2		
Constitutional Party	1		
		Last general election: March 1983	
Total	200	Next general election: March 1987	

PRODUCTION

Gross Domestic Product 1985 (Mk. million)	326 226	Gross Domestic Product by industry in 1984	
GDP per head, US dollars, 1985	10 751	(per cent):	
Gross fixed capital formation 1985 (Mk. million)	79 130	Agriculture and forestry	8
		Industry and construction	34
		Commerce	10
		Transport and communication	7
		Services	41

THE PUBLIC SECTOR

Public consumption 1985, per cent of GDP	20.0	General government revenue and expenditure, 1985	
Gross fixed capital formation 1985, per cent of GDP:		(Mk. million):	
General government	3.1	Current revenue	135 946
		Current expenditure	125 419
		of which:	
		Consumption	67 467
		Transfers	41 664
		Subsidies	10 279
		Interest on public debt	6 009

FOREIGN TRADE

Exports of goods and services, per cent of GDP, 1985	29.2	Imports of goods and services, per cent of GDP, 1985	28.1
Main exports in 1985 (per cent of total merchandise exports):		Main imports in 1985 (per cent of total merchandise imports):	
Agricultural and forestry products	2.8	Raw materials, etc.	62.5
Wood products	8.0	Fuels and lubricants	6.7
Pulp and paper	29.8	Investment goods	14.3
Metal products	29.0	Consumer goods	15.9
Other goods	30.4	Other	0.6

THE CURRENCY

Monetary unit: Markka		Currency units per US $, average of daily figures:	
		Year 1985	6.20
		March 1986	5.20

Note: An international comparison of certain basic statistics is given in an annex table.
1. Includes former Liberal People's Party.

INTRODUCTION

Finnish economic developments in recent years displayed many positive features which have attracted attention abroad. This holds true not the least for the high and stable growth of output and employment by European standards. It has been possible to contain both the budget and current external account deficits at sustainable levels and, thus, to avoid a large build-up of public and external debt. Moreover, inflation – though somewhat belatedly – has come down towards the OECD average. At the same time, however, certain underlying problems of the Finnish economy have emerged. Through 1985, the continued worsening of external competitiveness and export performance resulted in a further edging up of unemployment and this has become a focus in the policy debate.

While the marked fall in energy prices is likely to affect world trade positively, and hence buoy up Finnish exports to Western markets, the OECD projections for 1986 and 1987 point to the possibility of a deflection from the stable path of output growth which has characterised the 1980s so far, and to the likelihood of a continuing external disequilibrium. A recent fiscal package, aimed at lowering the cost in the tradeable goods sector, may help to reduce such risks. Part of the problem lies in the expected decline in exports to Eastern markets. Part I of the Survey reviews the key performance indicators in the first half of the 1980s and presents the outlook for the next eighteen months.

Macroeconomic policies have played an important role, both directly and indirectly, in stabilising growth since the second oil shock. Initiated with the 1977/82 stabilisation programme, economic policy has been formulated explicitly in a medium-term framework. Fiscal policy, within the requirement of being financially neutral over the cycle, has played an active role in stabilising the growth of output. Parallel to the shift towards a longer time horizon in fiscal planning, monetary, exchange rate and incomes policies have been directed towards breaking the so-called "devaluation cycle". Part II of the Survey discusses the restrictions on demand and supply management imposed by the recent "hard markka" policy and assesses policies and structural adaptation necessary to keep up the favourable economic performance in the years ahead. It concludes that the maintenance of a stable exchange rate requires not only a credible macroeconomic policy setting but also a high degree of supply-side flexibility. One aspect of the latter is taken up in Part III, where structural features of the Finnish labour market are analysed. The main conclusion which emerges is that while wages are flexible compared with most other OECD countries, certain institutional features introduce a number of rigidities in labour markets, thus making it difficult to reduce the rate of unemployment. Part IV offers some policy conclusions.

I. THE FINNISH ECONOMY AT THE CROSSROADS: TRENDS IN THE 1980s AND PROSPECTS

This part of the Survey addresses the issue of whether Finland, in the next couple of years, can be in a position to sustain the comparatively favourable economic performance observed in the past half decade. First the broad features of economic developments in the 1980s are recalled, stressing what may be perceived as underlying impediments to growth. Then, after discussing the implications of the "reverse" oil shock, projections for 1986 and 1987 are presented.

Key features of the 1980s

Stability of output and employment growth. Perhaps the most significant change in economic performance in the 1980s compared to the experiences of the 1970s has been the stability of business activity. The opening years of this decade – 1980 and 1981 – were still characterised by cyclical instability due at first to highly expansionary policies pursued in 1978/79 and subsequently to the second oil shock and international recession. But in the four years to 1985 cyclical variations, which in the past were typically larger than in most OECD countries, have virtually disappeared with annual rates of real GDP growth hardly deviating from 3 per cent. This rate is ½ percentage point below the estimated potential rate of growth and 1 per cent below the average growth rate over the last twenty-five years. Although, compared to the trend of the 1970s, productivity growth has decelerated for the total economy in the 1980-85 period because of the increase in the share of services in GDP, manufacturing productivity growth has accelerated, from 4 per cent to over 5 per cent per year (Table 1).

Table 1. **Potential and actual output growth and productivity**[1]

Average annual change, per cent

	1971-1974	1975-1979	1980-1985
Potential GDP, volume	5.4	2.9	3.4
Actual GDP, volume	4.9	2.3	3.2
Productivity, manufacturing	4.6	3.6	4.8
Productivity, total economy	5.1	3.5	3.2

1. Per man-hour.
Source: Submission from the Bank of Finland, National accounts.

Part of the explanation for comparatively rapid and balanced output growth in the first half of this decade lies in the active pursuit of countercyclical demand-management policies which contrasts markedly with the procyclical policy impact in the past enforced by the external constraint (see Part II). Other stabilising elements have been the changing structure of foreign trade as well as of domestic demand:

- The exposure to external disturbances diminished with the declining share of the timber, pulp and paper industry ("flex-price" sector) in total export earnings (55 per

8

cent in 1970 versus 38 per cent in 1985), as price developments and demand for these products are cyclically very sensitive and fluctuate more than world trade volumes and prices on average. The counterpart has been a growing share of the metal and engineering industry (or "fix-price" sector), increasing from 19 per cent to 31 per cent over the last fifteen years.

- The rapidly growing share of trade with the Soviet Union in the years 1979-82 supported the Finnish tradeable goods sector at a time when Western export markets were growing slowly or even shrinking in the aftermath of the second oil shock[1].
- The strength of the U.S. and Canadian dollars protected (at least until 1985) raw-material producing sectors, notably timber, pulp and paper, from North American competition. Favourable export revenue effects were also felt by exporters to the Soviet Union with the rouble tending to follow the dollar exchange rate.
- The pick-up in economic activity since the 1981 growth recession has been led by consumption, private as well as public, while cyclically more volatile demand elements such as investment and net real exports have fluctuated more moderately than in the past.

Smooth growth of output since the second oil shock has been associated with a relatively strong expansion of employment, despite better productivity growth than observed abroad. Indeed, Finland is among the few countries where the employment/population ratio was higher in 1984 than in 1970[2]. As in other OECD countries, it is mainly the service sector which has absorbed the growth in the labour force – with about three-quarters of the increase in the public sector (Table 2)[3]. Employment in construction remained until 1984 at the level of the late 1970s partly because of a shift towards more labour-intensive repair work. In parallel with trends elsewhere, the share of industrial employment declined through the 1980s but less than that in other Member countries, and employment levels still exceed the average of the preceding decade[4]. Nevertheless, the rate of unemployment has been on balance broadly unchanged at around 6 per cent for the last five years. This "stickiness" reflects a strong growth of the labour force owing to a continuing rise in the participation rates (which have stagnated on average in the OECD area since 1980) as well as to a boost to population growth by a return of migrants, notably from Sweden[5]. But, as discussed in Part III below, the high level of unemployment is also related to various rigidities in the labour market.

Table 2. **Trends in employment**

	1 000 persons			Average annual change, per cent	
	1976	1980	1985	1976-1980	1980-1985
Agriculture and forestry	367	314	280	–3.8	–2.3
Industry[1]	602	627	597	1.0	–1.0
Construction	187	176	179	–1.5	0.3
Trade, finance, insurance	450	455	509	0.3	2.3
Transport, storage, communications	173	184	186	1.6	0.2
Services[2]	486	562	680	3.7	3.9
Other	13	10	6	..	..
Total	2 278	2 328	2 437	0.5	1.2

1. Mining, manufacturing, electricity.
2. According to National Accounts employment data, the share of public sector employment was 70 per cent in 1984 and 64 per cent in 1976.
Source: Central Statistics Office.

Sectoral financial balances. Stable economic growth in recent years has been accompanied by a sustainable pattern of relative financial positions. The general government net lending position has deteriorated since the early 1970s, and deficits have emerged recently, though on a very moderate scale by international standards (Diagram 1)[6]. This deterioration has, however, been more than offset by an overall improvement of the aggregate financial position of the private sector, which composed:

- A trend increase in net lending of the financial sector reflecting, among other things, the growing funds associated with the private statutory pension scheme (TEL);

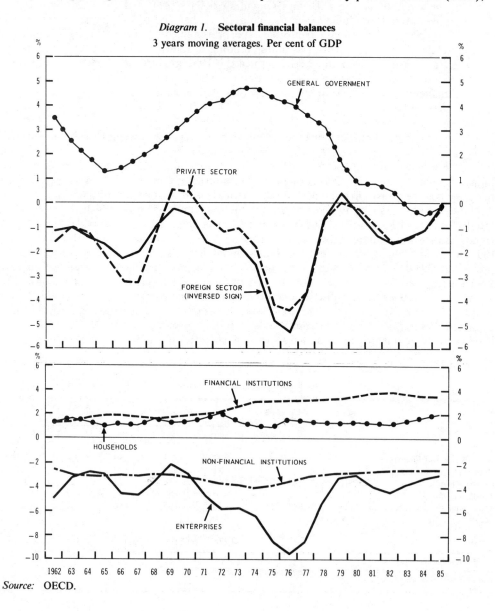

Diagram 1. **Sectoral financial balances**

3 years moving averages. Per cent of GDP

Source: OECD.

10

- A stabilisation in the 1980s of the corporate sector's financial deficit at lower levels than observed in the past, reflecting a restoration of average profitability after 1977/78 to its historical average, and a decline in the ratio of business investments to GDP (see below).

As a result, net lending by the foreign sector – i.e. the current external deficit – has been more moderate and fluctuated less than previously. One of the striking features compared to developments in the 1970s is an improved "trade-off" between the activity differential and net real exports (Diagram 2). In contrast to the 1970s, where higher economic activity levels in Finland than abroad were typically associated with negative real net export growth, it has been possible in the 1980s to maintain faster economic growth than the OECD average with less deterioration in the real foreign balance. This, in part, reflects lagged effects of the devaluations in 1977/78 and 1982.

Diagram 2. **Activity differentials and the real trade balance**

Percentage changes

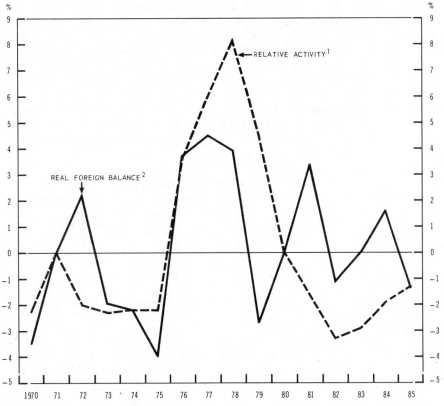

1. Relative activity is calculated as the real GDP deviation from trend in Finland's main trading partners minus the real GDP deviation from trend in Finland.
2. The contribution of real net exports to GDP volume growth.
Source: Submission from the Bank of Finland.

11

Impediments to medium-term growth. Along with the relatively favourable growth performance without severe financial disequilibria, there has been a number of less encouraging features, which, if not dealt with properly, could act as obstacles to the achievement of a high and stable growth of output in the future:

- A certain inertia in domestic cost and price trends poses a threat to international competitiveness;
- There has been a decline in the share of gross fixed investment in GDP, which over the medium term may at "face value" tend to reduce the economy's growth potential. But there has, on the other hand, been an increase in outlays on intangible investments such as R&D and marketing;
- Incentives to structural adjustment seem to have been weakened by the balancing role played by trade with the Soviet Union and the competititive advantage enjoyed by some sectors due to the strong dollar, though there are by now indications that the production structure in the metal and engineering industry is better adapted to the demand in Western markets.

Inflation performance has been less satisfactory than hoped for. Though the average pace of price increases (measured by the rise in the consumer price index) was slower in the first half of the 1980s than in the preceding decade, Finland has lost the favourable inflation differential vis-à-vis the OECD average which developed in the last years of the 1970s (Table 3). While Finland has participated in the area-wide process of disinflation in the 1980s – with a temporary pause following the 1982 devaluation – it was only in 1985 that there was a significant move towards closing the inflation gap. This was mainly due to a comparatively greater impact on the Finnish price performance of weaker raw material prices, although lower wage inflation, and lately more moderate increases in officially set food prices, also contributed. With actual real growth of output somewhat below its potential, general demand pressure would not appear to have exerted any positive influence on inflation. The main

Table 3. **Relative inflation performance**

	1973-1975	1975-1977	1977-1979	1979-1981	1981-1983	1983-1985
	Average annual change in private consumption deflator, per cent					
Finland	17.8	12.7	7.8	11.7	9.1	7.1
OECD	11.4	8.0	7.9	10.5	6.9	5.0
Inflation differential	+6.4	+4.7	−0.1	+1.2	+2.2	+1.9
	Contributions to the growth of consumer prices[1] (percentage points)					
Contributing factors:						
Wages	11.6	8.8	4.4	7.6	6.5	5.6
Productivity	−1.4	−0.8	−1.4	−1.4	−0.8	−1.0
Import prices	5.7	1.4	2.1	3.7	1.8	1.5
Food prices	3.0	3.2	1.6	1.7	2.0	1.3
Net direct taxes	−1.3	0.4	0.5	0.2	−0.2	0.6
Other factors	0.2	−0.2	0.5	−0.2	−0.2	−0.9
Total	17.8	12.7	7.8	11.7	9.1	7.1

1. Implicit private consumption deflator. Contributions calculated from the estimated price equation reported in Annex II.
Source: OECD.

difficulty seems to have been to bring wage inflation sufficiently under control, despite the extensive use of incomes policies (see Part III). A standard econometric analysis of price developments over the past fifteen years, described in Annex II, relates consumer price inflation to nominal labour cost changes, productivity growth, imports and food price developments. The results confirm conventional "rules of thumb" that within a year: a 1 per cent increase in nominal labour cost raises prices by ½ per cent; a 1 per cent change in productivity growth reduces inflation by ½ per cent; a 1 per cent rise in the prices of imported goods raises the price level by about ¼ per cent and a 1 per cent change in food prices is reflected as nearly ⅕ per cent higher inflation, though with a somewhat longer lag[7]. Although nominal wage growth has slowed in the 1980s, there still exists too much "nominal inertia" (see Part III) and hence domestic cost pressures from an international competitiveness point of view.

Wage-setting in Finland has often been described along the lines of the so-called Scandinavian model, where inflationary disturbances originating abroad are transmitted to the domestic economy via the wage leadership of the tradeable goods sector. However, this relationship may have changed since the first oil shock with the unemployment rate tripling and the labour market becoming more segmented (see Part III). A notable feature of the 1980s has been a tendency for the sheltered sector to provide initial impulses to domestic inflation. The reversal of the traditional direction of influence and strengthened wage-wage links pose an obvious threat to competitiveness of the export sector and may in part explain the inability to keep Finnish wage cost developments in line with increases abroad, despite a

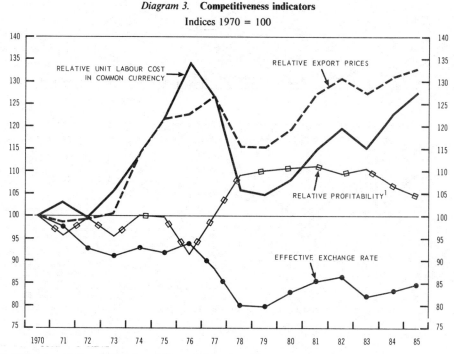

Diagram 3. **Competitiveness indicators**

Indices 1970 = 100

1. Relative export prices divided by relative unit labour costs.
Source: OECD Secretariat.

Diagram 4. **Sectoral investment trends**

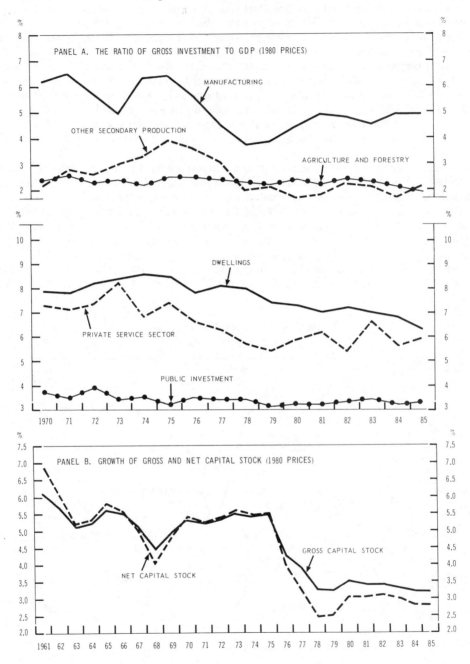

PANEL A. THE RATIO OF GROSS INVESTMENT TO GDP (1980 PRICES)

MANUFACTURING

OTHER SECONDARY PRODUCTION

AGRICULTURE AND FORESTRY

DWELLINGS

PRIVATE SERVICE SECTOR

PUBLIC INVESTMENT

PANEL B. GROWTH OF GROSS AND NET CAPITAL STOCK (1980 PRICES)

GROSS CAPITAL STOCK

NET CAPITAL STOCK

Source: National Accounts, Statistical Central Office, Ministry of Finance.

14

relatively better productivity performance (Diagram 3). The risk of compromising competitiveness may have acted as an incentive to reducing nominal wage inflation. However, the dissuasive potency of this factor has been reduced to the extent that the problem has been alleviated by the use of incomes policy (see Part II). More generally, certain institutional features provided little incentive to resist inflationary pressures[8]:

- The administration of price controls has been carried out, *inter alia,* through contacts with representative industry organisations whose primary task is to safeguard the interest of their overall membership rather than that of the most efficient firms (which nonetheless typically benefit most). More recently, measures have been taken to reduce official price controls and restrictive business practices;
- The system of agricultural price setting where the "cost plus" pricing procedure reduces incentives to save costs[9];
- The stickiness of raw material prices in forestry[10];
- The deductibility of interest payments from taxable income tends to make people less concerned with inflation;
- Tax scale adjustments have helped to moderate wage claims in the bargaining process. But the frequent use of this instrument has tended to weaken the discipline in wage negotiations as such adjustment have often been anticipated.

Although *total fixed investment* has grown in line with real output in recent years, the level is low by historical standards. The share of real private fixed investment in GDP fell to 22 per cent in the 1980s from 25 per cent and 27 per cent in the 1960s and early 1970s, respectively. A decline has been recorded in virtually all sectors, though it has been particularly pronounced in residential construction and non-manufacturing production sectors (Diagram 4). Industrial investment in plant and equipment has in part been replaced by increased R&D expenditure and buoyant direct investment abroad. Moreover, there has been a gradual slimming of the excess of the rates of return on investment in real assets over that on financial investments, which discouraged fixed capital formation in the current "high real interest rate era" (see Part III). However, it should not be forgotten that high real interest rates tend to increase required returns and hence the quality of investments. Parallel to the lower corporate investment activity, continuing cost pressures have induced a process of capital deepening rather than widening, reducing the future "employment potential" of the manufacturing sector (see Part III). The counterpart to the decline of the investment-to-GDP ratio has been a consumption-led pick-up of economic activity since the 1981 growth recession[11].

Incentives to a rapid pace of *structural adjustment* which characterised the 1970s weakened in the 1980s when the strong dollar and high oil prices favoured several open sector branches where "economic fundamentals" like world capacity, growth of world demand and entrance of new producers with considerably lower cost levels had otherwise dictated a continuing need for structural adjustment. A constant market share analysis reveals that the Finnish export performance was adversely affected by structural factors (to the tune of − 2½ per cent per year in the 1979-84 period, one-third being due to product patterns and two-thirds to the country composition)[12]. These features are as disquieting as in the Danish export performance, but considerably worse than observed in Sweden and Norway. Diagram 5 shows increasing market shares in traditional branches where growth of demand has been slower on average than for total OECD imports. Typically, market share gains coincide with devaluations of the Finnish markka, which, however, proved unable to reverse the worsening trend in overall export performance. This would seem to support the view that devaluations have to a large extent restored market positions of traditional branches and retarded the restructuring of the open sector towards rapidly growing markets.

Diagram 5. **Export performance**
Indices 1960 = 100

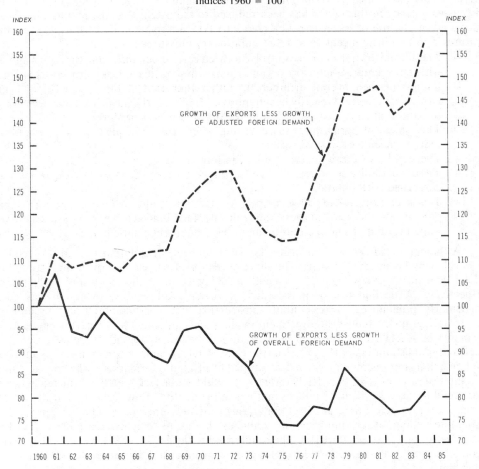

1. Adjusted for the commodity and country composition effects as calculated by the constant market share method.
Source: Submission from Bank of Finland.

A more disaggregated analysis reveals several problem areas (see Annex I, Diagram 1)[13] in traditionally important export sectors and in branches favoured by buoyant Soviet trade. Industries, which in the 1978-84 period grew less than their constant market share would imply, cover wood products, basic metals, furniture, textiles and textile raw materials and ships. Indeed, prospects for Soviet trade currently appear rather depressed and in view of the difficulty of switching sales from Eastern to Western markets in the short run, structural problems may again become rather severe in coming years. On the other hand, a promising export performance can be found in some high-tech areas such as professional, scientific and control instruments and electronic equipment.

Recent trends and the outlook for 1986 and 1987

The implications of the reverse oil shock. Falling energy prices since the turn of the year have in many respects altered the outlook for the Finnish economy, though for a number of structural reasons the effects are somewhat different from those observed internationally. In short, while Finland was less severely hit by oil price increases in the past than other countries, she is not likely to benefit from the oil price decline to the same extent either. Simulations with the OECD's INTERLINK model suggest that for the average OECD country a 10 per cent decline in the price of oil should increase real GDP growth by ¼ percentage point and decrease inflation by ½ percentage point relative to the baseline. With the assumed oil prices of $20 per barrel in the first half of 1986 and $15 per barrel in the rest of the projection period, a cautious application of the above "rule of thumb" implies a ½ to 1 per cent higher growth and 1½ to 2 per cent lower inflation for the OECD area as a whole. In the case of Finland, the effects of lower oil prices on total demand and output are likely to be muted by the special nature of the trade relationship with the Soviet Union, where the oil price fall is likely to result in a nearly proportionate fall in Finnish exports to this country[14]. Even so, the net terms-of-trade gains associated with the lower oil prices are large (of the order of 1½ per cent of GDP) and the impact on consumer prices (estimated to be some 2 percentage points in 1986) is also significant. Prospects for the world economy have improved in several respects, as reported in *Economic Outlook 39,* May 1986. The forecast growth of activity and demand has been revised upwards for most Member countries and so has the growth of Western export markets (Table 4). However, taking into account the decrease in purchasing power of OPEC and several developing countries, the growth of Western markets is now expected to slow down from 6¼ per cent in 1985 to 3½ per cent and 2¾ per cent in 1986 and 1987, respectively. The balancing requirement in bilateral trade with the Soviet Union, where Finnish imports mainly consist of energy, will importantly reduce exports to this country, though the built-in flexibility in the financing arrangements may delay the main negative effects on Finnish exports to 1987[15]. In total, the Finnish export market growth is assumed to decelerate from 5¾ per cent in 1985 to ½ per cent in 1986 and 1 per cent next year.

Table 4. **International assumptions**

Per cent change, year on year

	1985	1986	1987
Real GDP growth, OECD area	3½	3	3
Real domestic demand, OECD area	4	3½	3¼
Growth of export markets	5¾	½	1
of which:			
Western markets	6¼	3½	2¾
Eastern markets	1½	−9½	−6¼
Dollar price per barrel of oil	26.5	17½	15

Source: OECD.

Economic policy assumption. The OECD projections are based on the assumption that the present mix of fiscal and monetary policies is maintained throughout the next eighteen months. Concerning *fiscal policy,* the initial 1986 State Budget (prepared in autumn 1985) was intended to support the economy in anticipation of a cyclical downturn, as well as to moderate wage demand mainly through reduced taxation both to households and firms (see Annex III for details) (Table 5). However, with the new situation created by the fall in energy prices the Government has introduced a "differentiated energy tax package" which, while keeping the overall level of energy taxation unchanged, increases the cost of final energy use for agriculture and households, but lowers the tax burden for industry. This should improve cost competitiveness, perhaps to the equivalent of 2 per cent of the wage bill. The net impact of various tax measures is estimated to increase real household disposable income by ¾ per cent in 1986. *Monetary policy* in 1985 was mainly directed towards promoting the

Table 5. **Central government budget**

Markka million

	Cash flow estimate 1985	Cash forecast 1986	Change per cent
Total taxes	73 870	78 350	6
of which:			
Income and property taxes	25 750	27 805	8
Sales taxes	25 780	28 625	11
Taxes on import	1 640	1 710	4 ¼
Excise duties	12 695	12 585	−1
Other taxes	8 005	7 625	−4 ¾
Other revenue	11 200	12 150	8 ½
Long-term borrowing	10 720	12 360	15 ½
Total revenue	95 790	100 860	7 ½

			Change in volume, per cent
Consumption	24 570	26 450	2 ½
of which:			
Wages, salaries, pensions	14 470	15 650	1 ½
Transfer expenditure	50 190	53 910	2 ½
of which:			
State aid to local government	21 650	23 350	2 ½
Real investment	5 260	5 760	5 ½
Financial investment	3 700	3 920	2
Other expenditure	11 760	12 415	5 ½
of which:			
Interest expenditure on government debt	4 500	4 515	½
Total expenditure	95 480	102 455	3
Memorandum items:			
Net financial requirement as per cent of GDP	−0.8	−1.1	
State debt, billion Markka	47.0	51.0	
of which:			
Foreign debt	25.7	..	
State debt as per cent of GDP	13.9	14.0	

Source: Ministry of Finance.

18

process of disinflation. It proved possible to use the room for manœuvre given by lower international interest rates to allow a downward adjustment of domestic rates but only by an amount insufficient to prevent a further upward move of real interest rates. In view of the likely unfavourable development of the current external account it is assumed that the monetary authorities will ensure that real interest rates remain at their present high levels throughout the forecast period.

Wage assumptions and competitiveness. The average growth in manufacturing hourly wage costs decelerated by ½ percentage point in 1985 to 7¾ per cent, well above the rates of increase observed in most competititor countries. Also, the outcome of the spring wage negotiations suggests that wage moderation in Finland will continue to lag behind developments abroad. With contractual wage increases of 2½ per cent for 1986 as well as for 1987, and taking into account the carry-over, the shortening of the working week and wagedrift, the latter being relatively constant at around 2 to 2½ per cent, total hourly wage costs in manufacturing are assumed to increase by about 6½ per cent this year and 6¼ per cent in 1987. Despite the likelihood of a continuing favourable relative productivity performance, this implies that the cost competitiveness of the open sector, measured in local currencies, will not improve during the projection period (Table 6). This may be partly offset by the cost-reducing effects of the energy package, which are assumed to be evenly spread between 1986 and 1987. But, the lagged effects of past losses in competitiveness should still be felt on export performance, particularly in 1986.

Table 6. **Wage assumptions and competitiveness**

Per cent change, year on year

	1983	1984	1985	1986	1987
1. Hourly wage cost increase, manufacturing	10.0	9.0	7.7	6 ½	6 ¼
2. Productivity growth, manufacturing	6.0	5.8	3.5	3 ¼	3 ¼
3. Unit labour cost	3.4	4.3	5.2	3 ¼	3
4. Effective exchange rate change[1]	−5.8	1.1	1.1	−1 ½	0
5. Unit labour cost in common currency (3 + 4)	−2.6	5.5	6.3	1 ¾	3
Relative unit labour cost in common currency (Finland/OECD[1])	−4.4	+5.0	+2.9	−1	1.2

1. Includes fifteen competitor countries, based on double-weighting. See *OECD Economic Outlook 38,* Sources and Methods.
Source: OECD.

Business confidence. According to the April 1986 Business Tendency Survey, Finnish industry has reacted with some moderate optimism to the reverse oil shock. However, even with the announced energy cost reductions and the anticipation of some revival of demand in Western markets, the balance of confidence is still dominated by weak expectations of profitability and the inevitable downward adjustment of exports to the Soviet Union. The Survey foresees a declining rate of capacity utilisation, weak total export performance, but moderate growth of production and some increase in order stock. By branches, negative expectations of the immediate future are found in metal, construction and wood industries, whereas in the paper and pulp industry the near future is viewed with greater confidence. However, the June 1986 Investment Survey of the Bank of Finland suggests, that the confidence of the industry has somewhat improved in last few months.

Domestic demand, imports and exports

Total domestic demand increased about 4½ per cent in 1985, or three times as fast as in the previous year (Table 7). Much of it can be explained by the strong growth of private consumption, but an unexpectedly high contribution came from rapidly growing public consumption expenditures. Real disposable income of households increased by some 2½ per cent despite higher taxation, rising interest payments on consumer debt and a decrease in the number of self-employed. Although real interest rates were rising, the saving ratio declined slightly, as entrepreneurial incomes, normally associated with a lower spending propensity, grew only little. Preliminary statistics suggest that public consumption, despite expenditure controls, increased strongly in 1985 (volume growth of 4¼ per cent) partly due to certain defense deliveries. Also, the continuing strength of local government real consumption suggests that spending control has still a long way to go to be effective. Further disinflation in 1986 may boost private consumption through real balance and wealth effects. Real disposable income of households could increase no less than 4½ per cent because of new wage settlements and the income tax adjustment. The gain from disinflation and the adjustment of tax scales will decrease in 1987 and the saving ratio is assumed to continue rising. On this basis, the volume of private consumption is likely to grow by 3 per cent next year compared to 4 per cent

Table 7. **Short-term prospects**

	Markka billion	Per cent change from previous year, volume		
	1984	1985	1986	1987
A. Demand and output				
Private consumption	164.7	3.2	4	3
Public consumption	59.7	4.3	3	2 ¼
Gross fixed investments	72.4	3.1	1	1
Final domestic demand	296.8	3.4	3	2 ½
Stock formation	3.8	1.0	0	0
Total domestic demand	300.6	4.4	3	2 ½
Exports of goods and services	95.6	0.3	0	¼
Imports of goods and services	87.8	5.1	3 ¼	2 ¼
Foreign balance	7.8	−1.5	−1	−½
GDP	308.3	2.8	2	2
Industrial production		3.0	2	2 ¼
Unemployment (rate)		6.3	6 ¾	7
B. Prices and wages				
GDP deflator		6.5	3 ½	3 ½
Private consumption deflator		5.9	3	3 ¼
Hourly wage cost in industry		8.5	6 ½	6 ¼
		Dollars billion		
C. Balance of payments				
Trade balance (BoP basis)		0.9	1.5	1.5
Balance of services		−0.4	−0.7	−0.7
Net invisibles		−1.6	−2.1	−2.2
Current balance		−0.6	−0.6	−0.7
Memorandum item:				
Current balance, Markka billion		−4.0	−3.3	−3.8

Source: OECD.

this year. Public consumption growth is projected to decelerate this year and next, in part to match the revenue loss from lower taxation. Following a rather moderate revival in 1985[16], gross fixed investment is expected to increase cumulatively by 2 per cent in volume in the two years to 1987. All in all, total domestic demand growth may decelerate to 3 per cent in 1986 and to 2½ per cent in 1987.

As noted above, Finnish export performance was disappointing last year. In the autumn it was still generally expected that the volume of exports would grow by about 4 per cent in 1985. The outcome was, however, only ½ per cent because of a sharp deceleration in the second half of the year. With a 5¾ per cent market growth for Finnish exports, market shares were lost in 1985 at twice the pace experienced in previous years (and notably in Western markets). The volume of goods exports to the East grew by 17 per cent in 1985, while that to the West declined by about 2 per cent. The falling dollar and commodity prices in world markets were felt by Finnish exporters and importers in 1985, but on a year-to-year basis foreign trade prices still rose by 2¾ per cent and the terms of trade remained unchanged. In the forecast for 1986/87, a key issue for export developments will be the effects of the oil price fall on bilateral Soviet trade. As noted above, the fall in oil prices is not expected to be felt to its full extent in the reduction of exports to the Soviet Union, especially in 1986[17]. The total volume of exports is forecast to remain flat in 1986 and to grow slightly in 1987, as the projected rise in total OECD trade will be largely offset by the deterioration of price competitiveness since 1984 (cumulatively by 8 per cent), although there will probably be efforts to fill the growing slack of capacity in the Eastern trade sector by increasing market shares in the West.

Output, employment and productivity

The steady 3 per cent growth path of production seems to have been broken in mid-1985. Total output expanded only 1 per cent (s.a.a.r.) in the second half of 1985 and in December 1985 industrial production was 2½ per cent lower than a year ago. For 1985 as a whole industrial output increased by 2½ per cent. Production increased strongly in the metal industry but fell in forestry. The level of activity in construction did not change, but in agriculture output was reduced sharply. Only in the service sector did output grow by 4 per cent in volume. The rather favourable overall growth performance in the 1980s, which was attained through expansionary policy and balancing effects of Soviet trade, has made it difficult to perceive the continuing need for structural adjustment.

In the present *OECD projections* the outlook for Finland is less favourable than suggested earlier. In 1986 and 1987 real GDP growth is expected to decelerate to 2 per cent, compared with an official projection of 2½ per cent. With the slowdown of production, unemployment began to increase rapidly in the second half of 1985, though this may be partly due to the reform of the unemployment insurance system taking effect in 1985, probably increasing the number of job seekers in labour market survey statistics. The rapid productivity growth in manufacturing is projected to continue in 1986 and 1987, increasing the absorption requirements for the service sector. Service sector employment is expected to grow, but unemployment is likely to rise in the projection period, although not quite to the peak level of the late 1970s. Over the medium term, demographic factors could mitigate the problem of unemployment[18].

Prices and costs

In 1985 the consumer price level was on average 5.9 per cent higher than in the previous year, but the increase slowed down to only 1½ at annual rate in the second half of the year, mainly reflecting weak world commodity prices and the falling dollar. The slackening in

21

domestic cost pressures has been much less impressive. Inflation is forecast to be halved in 1986, thanks to falling import prices, but the carry-over effect of labour costs, the likely wagedrift as well as the new wage settlements suggest that domestic cost pressures will remain high. In 1987 consumer price inflation may accelerate slightly, as import prices stop falling and wage cost pressure persists.

The balance of payments

After a rather good performance in 1984 with a trade surplus (BoP basis) amounting to a record level of 11.1 per cent of export revenues, the trade balance deteriorated in 1985 (halving the trade surplus to 6½ per cent of export revenues) as vigorous growth of domestic demand increased imports just as export growth came to a halt. The balance on services deteriorated also, as Finnish tourism spending abroad increased and freight revenues as well as income from project exports diminished. Interest payments on foreign debt remained high ($1.1 billion), although exchange rate changes reduced the net debt by as much as the current account deficit increased it (Table 8). At the end of 1985 the ratio of foreign debt to GDP was 16 per cent, 1½ percentage points lower than in the previous year. In 1986 and 1987, the trade balance is projected to improve, mainly due to the terms-of-trade gain in 1986. The current account deficit, however, is projected to remain at about 1 per cent of GDP. The lower dollar and possibly lower international interest rates alleviate the pressure on net investment income payments in 1986 but this could be offset by continuing deterioration of the services account. With brisk growth of household real incomes, especially that of pensioners, increased travelling abroad is likely and with the share of merchandise carried under the Finnish flag falling, the deficit in the service account (BoP basis) may move to a higher level and stay at that level for some time to come.

Table 8. **The balance of payments**
Dollars million

	1982	1983	1984	1985
Exports, fob	13 046	12 187	13 098	13 450
Imports, fob	12 808	12 036	11 607	12 534
Trade balance	238	151	1 491	916
– As per cent of GDP	0.5	0.3	2.9	1.7
Non-factor services, credit	2 771	2 637	2 522	2 341
Non-factor services, debit	2 553	2 539	2 718	2 716
Balance of non-factor services	218	98	–196	–375
– As per cent of GDP	0.4	0.2	–0.4	–0.7
Investment income, net	–1 131	–1 045	–1 130	–1 001
– As per cent of GDP	–2.2	–2.1	–2.2	–1.8
Private and official transfers, net	–134	–143	–165	–186
– As per cent of GDP	–0.3	–0.3	–0.3	–0.3
Current balance	–810	–940	0	–646
– As per cent of GDP	–1.6	–1.9	0	–1.2
Memorandum item:				
Net foreign debt as per cent of GDP, in local currency	16.7	17.8	16.5	15.0

Sources: OECD, Ministry of Finance.

II. THE EXCHANGE RATE REGIME
AND THE MACROECONOMIC POLICY MIX

The legacy from the 1970s

The macroeconomic policy pursued in recent years departs in several respects from the approach adopted in the 1970s and earlier[19]. A full review of stabilisation policies during the earlier period has been given in earlier OECD Surveys of Finland. In a somewhat stylised form the elements listed below may be distinguished, bearing in mind that economic policy in general gave priority to investment, economic growth, export competitiveness and rapid structural adjustment:

- *Fiscal policy* was constrained by relatively strict annual budget balance requirements and embodied a high degree of selectivity.
- *Monetary policy* was mainly aimed at keeping interest rates low to promote investment but the external constraint often induced sharp tightening of the supply of credit.
- *Incomes policy* was actively used to influence wage settlements, mainly by changes in taxation, but left largely unco-ordinated with other elements of macroeconomic policies.
- *Exchange rate policies* were directed towards safeguarding the competitiveness of Finnish industry, and with a view to offsetting real exchange rate appreciations which resulted from insufficient domestic cost control, major devaluations took place on several occasions: 1957 (28 per cent), 1967 (24 per cent) and 1977/78 (10 per cent).

In this policy setting, it is hardly surprising that demand-management policies had markedly procyclical effects on the economy (Diagram 6). This was particularly pronounced for *fiscal policy* which until the late 1970s was guided by the perceived need to balance outlays and revenues over the very short term. Moreover, since inflation was considered largely as a cost and labour market problem, the role of fiscal policy in damping price rises was mainly seen as being played through selective measures: considerable weight was given to the effect of fiscal measures on consumer price developments and income tax reductions were seen as contributing positively to the fight against tax-push inflation despite its stimulating effects on demand. Public spending was kept under relatively firm control[20]. In contrast to many other countries, expenditure control was deemed necessary to avoid deficit financing (and the associated "cash crises") rather than because of perceived adverse allocative effects of public spending. The institutional set-up for and implementation of *monetary policy* were reviewed in last year's Economic Survey of Finland[21]: suffice to note here the generally accommodating stance interrupted by a severe credit squeeze in 1975/76 as the balance of payments constraint became increasingly tight. Despite the intensive use of *incomes policies,* it is not evident that cost developments were more firmly under control than elsewhere. This was in part related to the accommodating monetary policy and the fact that, as noted above, throughout the post-war period the authorities took the main responsibility for maintaining international competitiveness largely through the exchange rate policy, and hence providing little incentives for economic agents to strive for nominal income moderation.

In sum, in a system where monetary and exchange rate policies accommodate wage increases the authorities, *de facto*, renounced exercising any inflation control. With competitiveness and hence employment and economic growth assured by the authorities

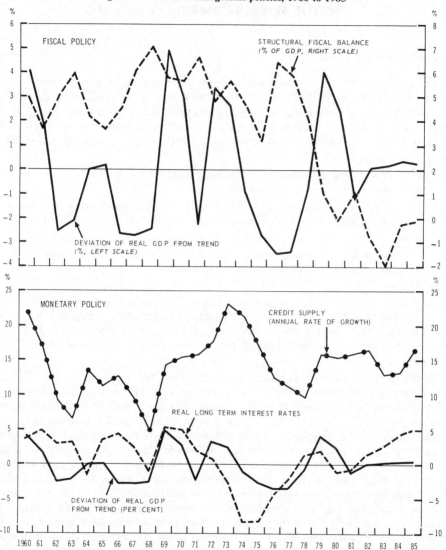

Diagram 6. **Demand management policies, 1960 to 1985**

Source: OECD.

through accommodating monetary and exchange rate policies, the policy approach appeared as if the authorities aimed at stabilising the real exchange rate at some suitable level over the medium term. Exchange rate depreciations, triggered by a certain cost-induced loss of international competitiveness, pushed up domestic costs. The more powerful such cost effects of exchange rate changes are, the more destabilising an accommodating policy stance would be for domestic prices. It is precisely in such circumstances that "vicious circle" mechanisms

24

Diagram 7. Key performance indicators

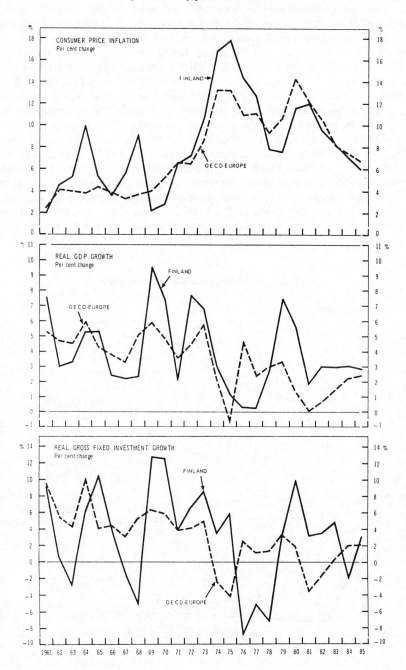

Source: OECD.

25

tended to arise, whereby inflation and devaluations acted to reinforce each other. This vicious circle may have been accentuated to the extent that expectations were adversely affected and/or the credibility of the government policy was at stake. It is therefore hardly surprising that Finland experienced sharper fluctuations in the rate of inflation, profit shares, investment and economic growth than observed elsewhere during the 1960s and 1970s (Diagram 7).

Diagram 8 illustrates the last points. Both the devaluations in 1967 and in 1977/78 improved competitiveness and profitability of industry significantly (the horizontal leftward movement of the curve) which subsequently stimulated production and employment. It was, however, followed by wage and price increases and deteriorating competitiveness and profitability. Hence, production fell back relative to developments elsewhere (the rightward movement of the curve). However, the evidence is not unambiguous. As can be seen from the diagram, each production cycle lies on a higher level than the previous one, though this may be the result of other exogenous factors. On the inflation side a similar cycle is detectable. Following each devaluation price competitiveness remained strong for a while. But the effects of rising import prices and the subsequent wage-price spiral prompted by increased profits and augmented by wage-wage links (wage earner attempting to maintain relative income shares) have eroded the initial gains in competitiveness and led to real exchange rate appreciation.

Diagram 8. **Industrial production and competitiveness**

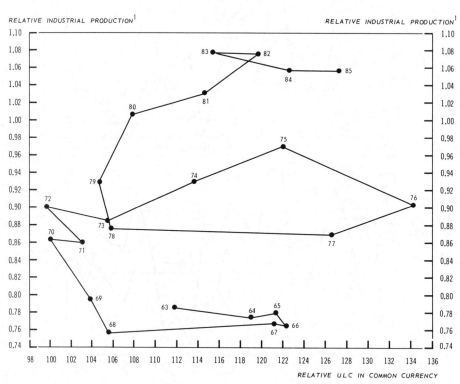

1. Industrial production in Finland relative to OECD Europe.
Source: OECD.

26

1980 to 1985: A quest for stability

With the adoption of the 1977/82 medium-term stabilisation programme, policy priorities seem to have gradually shifted from aiming at maximal economic growth and rapid structural change to a quest for a more stable economic environment. In particular, the wish to break with the devaluation cycles of the past, and thus secure the preconditions for smooth and sustainable economic growth and employment, meant that combatting inflation came to the forefront of policy design. Consequently, the rather rigid policy assignment and implementation rules of the past were progressively changed.

Fiscal policy. The innovation of the 1977/82 programme was, as noted above, to allow fiscal policy to play a more active role in stabilising the economy. The strict requirement for balancing the State budget each year was extended in time to cover the cycle (without any precise definition being given to the latter). The perception of greater room for manœuvre was also supported by the relatively small size of the public sector in relation to GDP and its low level of domestic indebtedness by international standards. According to OECD calculations of

Table 9. **Fiscal policy since 1982**

Per cent of GDP

	1982	1983	1984	1985	1986 official projection
General government revenues	38.4	37.4	39	40 ½	40
of which:					
Direct taxes	15.6	15.6	16.0	16 ½	16 ½
Indirect taxes[1]	14.9	14.0	14.6	14 ¾	14 ½
Social security contributions	4.5	4.4	4.8	5 ½	5
Other	3.4	3.5	3.6	3 ¾	3 ¾
General government expenditure	35.8	36.1	36.1	37 ¼	37 ½
of which:					
Consumption	19.0	19.3	19.4	20	20 ¼
Subsidies	4.1	3.3	3.2	3	3
Social security benefits	5.9	6.3	6.3	6 ½	6 ½
Social assistance[2]	3.6	3.8	3.8	4	4
Other	3.2	3.4	3.5	3 ¾	3 ½
Saving	2.6	1.3	2.9	3	2 ½
Consumption of fixed capital[3]	0.8	1.0	1	1	1
Gross capital formation	3.8	4.0	3.5	3 ½	3 ½
Financial surplus	–0.4	–1.8	0.3	½	–0
Effects of fiscal policy[4]	+2.1	+1.0	–1.6	–0.2	+0.6
of which:					
Central government	+1.2	+0.7	–1.7	–0.1	0.0
Local government	+0.5	+0.4	+0.1	+0.4	+0.5
Social security funds	+0.4	–0.1	–0.1	–0.1	+0.1
Change in structural budget balance[5]	+1.8	+1.2	–1.7	–0.2	+0.1

1. Includes compulsory fees and fines.
2. Includes other current transfers.
3. Includes net capital transfers.
4. Estimates of Ministry of Finance, + expansionary, – restrictive.
5. Estimates of OECD Secretariat, + expansionary, – restrictive.
Source: Ministry of Finance, OECD.

the cyclically-adjusted general government budget balance, three policy phases may be distinguished since 1980 (Table 9):

1982/83: A moderate fiscal *stimulus* was given to the economy to absorb the slack induced by the international recession;

1984/85: A somewhat *restrictive* stance was adopted as the international recovery and the domestic upswing got under way;

1985/86: A *neutral to expansionary* policy was decided as both the domestic economy and exports were expected to weaken.

An interesting feature of fiscal policy, which probably makes the Finnish experience deviate from other countries', is the high degree of selectivity in the use of tax instruments. The adjustment of tax brackets has often been closely connected with incomes policy settlements (1977/78, 1981, 1984 and 1986) apparently with greater success in shifting a lowered direct tax pressure onto nominal wage claims than in the past. Also, social security contributions have played a role in the effort to fine-tune cost and real income developments (see Part III). Moreover, the sales tax has on several occasions been adjusted with the view to affecting both investments and international competitiveness of specific sectors. More recently, a differentiated energy tax package proposed by the Government is intended, as noted above, to enhance industrial cost competitiveness, while leaving the overall burden of energy taxation unchanged. More striking, and more common to developments abroad, however, is the relatively rapid growth of cyclically-adjusted government spending, which in real terms expanded around 4 per cent since the turn of the decade (the annual rate of real growth was 5½ per cent in the 1970s). Indeed, the ratio of cyclically-adjusted public expenditure to GDP has risen with major leaps in the mid-1970s and in the early-1980s. The first was associated with the implementation of new welfare programmes and the second with the expansionary policy stance in 1981-82, subsequently followed by rapid local authority spending. The rise in the ratio of the overall taxation to GDP may also be separated into three periods. During the early 1970s the tax/GDP ratio increased mainly because of fiscal drag. In 1976 the tax burden increased because of the recession and new tax-financed unemployment programmes. Tax increases in 1984/85 reflected the countercyclical policy stance. The balance of these developments has been a rapid build-up of government indebtedness (with debt servicing increasingly crowding out other expenditure), though, at 14 per cent of GDP, its level is still low by international standards.

Monetary policy.   As could be expected, external considerations have been dominating the conduct of monetary policy in recent years. This has been reflected most significantly in interest rate policy, where interest rates progressively changed from being an end target to become the key instrument of policy with the ongoing deregulation of financial markets[22]. The tightening of monetary policy in 1983 was prompted not only by the need to discipline exchange market expectations in the aftermath of the 1982 devaluation but also by an excessive rate of domestic credit expansion. Despite a current external account equilibrium and a marked interest rate differential in favour of the markka, the exchange market held a rather dim view of prospects of maintaining the exchange rate, as the inflation differential compared to the OECD average widened through 1983. The result was considerable capital outflows and severe pressures on the exchange rate. To choke off such speculation, the call money rate was raised to 17½ per cent in late 1983. The opening of a wide interest rate differential vis-à-vis international capital markets and the disappearance of the domestic differential between the call money market and other unregulated domestic financial markets led to a reversal of capital flows (Diagram 7). Through 1984 and into early 1985, the key problem facing the monetary authorities was to sterilise capital inflows stimulated mainly by the portfolio adjustment of Finnish companies to the new yield structures following financial deregulation. It was thought necessary to counter the domestic liquidity impact of capital inflows, thus defending the higher level of domestic interest rates. This was done mainly in the form of intervention in the forward exchange market[23].

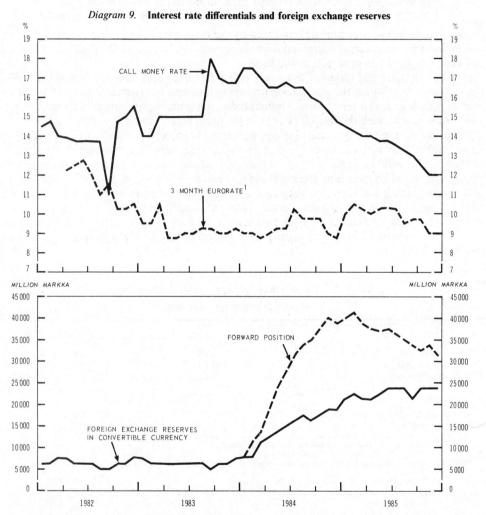

Diagram 9.   **Interest rate differentials and foreign exchange reserves**

1.   Euro currency interest rates weighted with their relative importance in the Finnish currency basket.
Source: Submission from Bank of Finland.

As from the latter part of 1984 and to May 1986 short-term interest rates were reduced gradually, reflecting the strength of the markka, the broad balance in external payments and the reduction of the international inflation differential. However, as incentives to import capital have diminished, the forward position of the Bank of Finland has been progressively reduced. Towards the turn of the year and into early 1986, there was some unwinding of external borrowing. This may reflect several influences:

- The reduced interest rate differential vis-à-vis international capital markets has weakened incentives to borrow abroad;
- The ban on sales of bonds and debentures to non-residents decided by mid-1985[24];
- The continuing interest of Finnish firms in investing abroad[25];
- Domestic investment activity and hence borrowing abroad was depressed;

To discourage speculative pressures induced by the Norwegian devaluation in May 1986, the call money rate was sharply increased for a short period in May, and the markka was allowed to depreciate by 2 per cent within the band.

While the external target of monetary policy has been met in recent years, the initially slow progress in bringing the disinflation process in line with international trends has required increasingly high real interest rates. Undoubtedly, the initial tightening of monetary policy in 1983/84 in unison with the similar change in the fiscal policy stance was justified to avoid the errors of the past in letting a "devaluation-generated" recovery get out of hand. On the other hand, higher real interest rates have in the short run acted as a brake on fixed capital formation and induced firms to invest in financial rather than real assets. However, as noted above, higher real interest rates may in the longer run have improved the quality of investment and by dampening the real exchange rate appreciation helped in attenuating the competitiveness weakness of the exposed sector. Domestic credit expansion accelerated in 1985 (though this in part reflected a switch to domestic sources of credit after the ban on sales of securities to non-residents), and fiscal policy moved progressively in a more expansionary direction (Table 10).

Table 10. **The growth of the money supply and bank lending**

Annual rate of growth, per cent

	1982	1983	1984	1985
Narrow money supply (M1)[1]	15.9	7.6	16.4	11.0
Broad money supply[2]	13.7	13.3	16.2	17.6
Bank lending[3]	18.1	14.1	14.5	18.4
Memorandum items:				
Real broad money supply[4]	4.1	4.0	6.6	10.4
Real bank lending[4]	8.1	4.7	5.0	11.2

1. M1 = Coins and notes in circulation plus demand deposits held by the public.
2. Broad money supply = M1 plus time deposits held by the public.
3. Bank lending = loans and bills in domestic currency plus overdraft credits plus domestic credits denominated in foreign currency.
4. Deflated by GDP deflator.
Source: Bank of Finland, OECD.

Exchange rate policies since the second oil crisis

The exchange rate regime. The regime adopted by the Bank of Finland since 1977 has been to maintain a stable currency index within a pre-announced range. The index has been calculated in relation to a trade-weighted basket of foreign currencies. The main rationale for a nominal exchange rate pegging, as in many other smaller Member countries, has been to minimise variations in the external value of the home currency and hence any detrimental effects which these fluctuations might have on the tradeable goods sector, given the small size of foreign exchange markets, the initial absence of forward facilities and the lack of capital flows motivated by conventional yield considerations[26]. The exchange rate, being a *relative* price, exerts important influences:

- Profitability of industries exposed to foreign competition is affected relative to other sectors. An undervalued exchange rate leads to increased profitability in the traded goods sector, inducing some industries to keep capacity even if underlying structural considerations suggest that it should contract. An overvalued exchange rate has opposite effects and may trigger sector demands for border protection or domestic support measures.
- To the extent that the current profitability influence expectations about the future, investment decisions may also be affected leading to over or under-investment in the tradeable goods sector, and hence a misallocation of fixed capital. Consequently, it becomes more difficult to adjust the structure of production when the exchange rate returns to a sustainable long-run level.
- More generally, external pressures for structural change, independently of their origin, are alleviated by an undervalued currency and exacerbated by an over-valuation. Thus, the exchange rate policy largely determines the permeability of the domestic economy to external pressures for adjustment, thereby importantly affecting the productivity trend in the tradeable goods sector and its overall competitive climate, in particular with regard to adopting new technologies.

The changing assignments.　　The role of the exchange rate policy within the overall stabilisation effort has changed gradually in recent years. The anti-inflation aspect of the exchange rate policy appears to have been given increasing weight. This has in part been based on a wider recognition of the inflationary bias of past policy assignments, given the special nature of the Finnish policy setting. Over the years from the late 1950s to the end of the 1970s, the exchange rate policy was mainly used to safeguard international competitiveness, combined with a *de facto* pro-cyclical fiscal policy and a largely accommodating monetary policy. The experience of the "devaluation cycles" during this period showed that while the beneficial impact of large devaluations on output, employment and the trade balance tended to be temporary, the effects on the price level were of a more lasting nature (see further below). Similarly, in 1973/74 when terms-of-trade developments effectively corresponded to a 40 per cent devaluation, the failure to revalue the markka or to offset the effects of the external inflationary shock by fiscal measures led to severe internal and external disequilibria. Following the second oil shock, and the simultaneous surge in inflation and unemployment there was in Finland as elsewhere a growing perception that a precondition for more stable output and employment growth was firmer control over domestic costs and prices. Hence, a greater emphasis was laid on incomes and exchange rate policy serving as an anchor for the evolution of costs and prices.

The first signs of the "new" exchange rate policy were seen in 1979 and 1980 when the markka was allowed to appreciate (for the first time in the post-war period) by a cumulative 5 per cent under conditions of an export boom and imminent domestic overheating. The decision to devalue the markka in two rounds by a total of 10 per cent at the time of the Nordic devaluations in 1982 did not as such represent a deviation from the key policy aim of a stable external value of the currency. Indeed, part of the efforts to restore the competitive position took the form of reduced social security contributions, which made it possible to depreciate the markka less than a strict krona parity would have required. The markka devaluation at that time was triggered off by the preceding cumulative 26 per cent depreciation of the Swedish krona (in 1981 and 1982) and as such "unavoidable" given the close economic links between the two countries and the similarities in the structure of exports (the high share of wood, pulp and paper in export earnings). A small appreciation of the markka took place in early 1984.

The choice of the relevant basket and the basic norm which guides the criteria according to which exchange rate policies are conducted is as important as discretionary exchange rate policies. The currency basket determined on the basis of trade-weights reflects the consideration that domestic price competitiveness should be protected against foreign currency action. However, such a "fixed-on-the-average" exchange rate does not prevent the economy from being highly vulnerable to foreign price disturbances. Such shocks are often an important source of macroeconomic fluctuations in economies like Finland where raw materials occupy a significant position in both exports and imports. A well-known example already cited above is the 1973/74 boom, when the behaviour of trade prices and their effects on the whole economy resembled that of a devaluation of the markka by some 40 per cent, though the markka was kept stable against a basket of currencies[27]. As the economy was already approaching capacity ceilings, the external shock in combination with initially

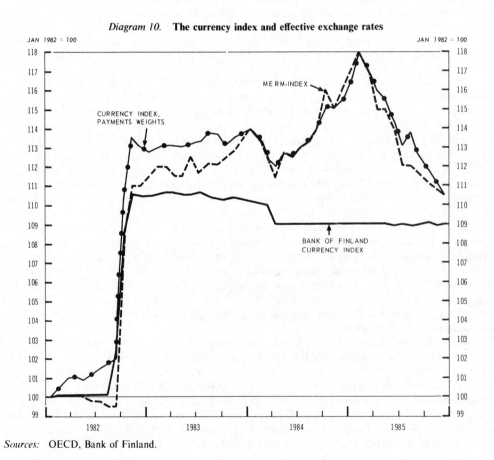

Diagram 10. **The currency index and effective exchange rates**

Sources: OECD, Bank of Finland.

32

expansionary policies soon led to overheating of the economy, an acceleration of inflation and loss of competitiveness, and a substantial deficit in the current account.

A more recent experience may illustrate another side of the problem of maintaining a currency basket. As noted above, apart from a small appreciation in March 1984, the currency index remained highly stable between 1983 and 1985. The measurement of effective exchange rates is however critically dependent on the weighting system, as can be seen from Diagram 10. Indeed, alternative weighting matrices indicate that in the year to March 1985, the effective exchange rate depreciated by more than 5 per cent largely due to the rise in the dollar, helping on the one hand to maintain activity in the tradeable goods sector and on the other to offset some of the disinflation influences coming from abroad[28]. This movement was reversed in 1985 as the effective exchange rate appreciated with the steady fall in the U.S. dollar. The improved competitiveness of North American producers in the timber, pulp and paper sector and the difficulty of domestic producers to reduce costs in parallel with the weakening of the dollar led to dramatic declines in exports and a severe profit squeeze in this sector. At the same time, the deceleration of inflation, measured e.g. by the consumer index, tended to exaggerate the degree to which the underlying rate of inflation had been brought under control.

III. ASPECTS OF SUPPLY-SIDE FLEXIBILITY:
THE LABOUR MARKET

The Finnish authorities aim at reducing both unemployment and inflation simultaneously. The feasibility of attaining these medium-term goals depends importantly on the functioning of the labour market, in particular the wage formation process. This part of the Survey examines various aspects of the Finnish labour market.

Issues related to wage flexibility

Nominal wage rigidity. Despite the historically high unemployment rates throughout the 1980s, it is only most recently that nominal wage increases have come down significantly from close to double-digit levels. This may indicate that wages, the most crucial element in the market-clearing process, are rather slow to adjust in Finland. However, estimated wage equations for a number of OECD countries suggest that, measured by the effect of the unemployment rate on money wages, wage flexibility in Finland is relatively high by international standards[29] (see Annex II). This may also explain why unemployment in Finland, though high by historical standards, has remained lower than in most European countries (except Austria, Sweden, Iceland and Norway).

One concept which is widely used in the analysis of wage behaviour is the so-called non-accelerating inflation rate of unemployment (NAIRU) (Table 11). Various national studies suggest that from the late 1950s to the early 1970s the NAIRU was around a 2¼ per cent level (Halttunen, Koskela-Wiren), although higher at the end of the period (Paunio-Suvanto). A decade later the rate had apparently increased to some 3½ to 4 per cent (Santamäki, Pehkonen, Kanniainen-Lilleberg, Tarkka) with a further rise taking place in the 1980s. These results are compatible with each other as well as with the results of the Secretariat, which for the late 1970s suggest a NAIRU at 3¾ to 4¼ per cent and about 5 per cent in the 1980s.

Table 11. **NAIRU estimates**

	Time period	Average unemployment rate	NAIRU estimates
		Per cent	
Phillips curve, Version A[1]	1976 I – 1979 II	5.8	3.8
	1980 I – 1985 I	5.7	5.2
Phillips curve, Version B[1]	1976 I – 1979 II	5.8	4.3
	1980 I – 1985 I	5.7	4.9

1. See Annex II for detailed specifications.
Source: OECD Secretariat.

Actual unemployment rates remained below any estimate of the NAIRU in the early 1970s but the situation has since been reversed[30]. On this basis, one could expect inflation pressures originating from labour markets to have diminished over the last decade. It is therefore surprising that the average growth of hourly earnings did not differ significantly between the two five-year periods, 1975-80 and 1980-85. However, there was a marked deceleration through the latter period from a peak of 12¾ per cent in 1981 to some 8½ per cent in 1985, with a further deceleration projected this year. Since unemployment in Finland is projected to remain above the estimated NAIRU, the effect of labour market conditions on nominal wage growth and inflation is likely to be negative also in the near future, increasing the room for manœuvre for demand management.

An important element in nominal wage behaviour has been employers' social security contributions which in Finland – as in Sweden and Norway – constitute a significant part of the total compensation of employees. Statutory payroll taxes in Finland are at about the average international level and they have been actively used as a tool of incomes policy since the latter part of the 1970s. Previously the share of non-wage labour cost in total compensation of employees had increased sharply, from some 14 per cent in 1970 to 18 per cent in 1976, thus contributing importantly to the observed widening in the real labour cost gap (see below). However, in incomes policy settlements since 1978, payroll taxes have been steadily reduced[31]. The statutory contribution rate for public social security schemes was reduced from 9¼ per cent of the wage bill in 1976 to 8 per cent in 1985. The contribution to the private pension insurance scheme (TEL), notwithstanding the permanent upward pressure of premiums, was 11.5 per cent in 1985, still below its 1977 level. The frequent adjustment of payroll taxes has been a factor in increasing both nominal and real wage flexibility. Indeed, inclusion of the employers' social security contribution rate in econometrically estimated wage equations provides some evidence of a backward shifting to nominal wages.

Real wage flexibility. The matching of demand and supply in the labour market depends more directly on flexibility of *real* wages, which comprises the responsiveness of nominal wages to unemployment as well as to prices. As noted, nominal wages respond significantly to labour market slack in Finland. On the other hand, their short-run response to prices has been estimated to be rather small. The econometric evidence thus lends strong support to the view that a high degree of real wage flexibility exists in Finland, a degree of flexibility which is comparable to that in the United States on the basis of a widely-used indicator[32]. Part of this is explained by the bargaining behaviour of unions which, unlike in most other countries, often explicitly announce their wage demands on the basis of

34

productivity growth. In this particular respect, the Finnish wage formation process resembles that of Germany and Switzerland[33].

An alternative characterisation of the wage formation process is one where the natural rate – an equilibrium rate of unemployment – tends to adjust to the actual level of unemployment. This so-called hysteresis hypothesis receives empirical support in the estimates reported in Annex II. Indeed, specifications of Finnish wage equations, while confirming the above findings of real wage flexibility, show that *changes* in the rate of unemployment, perhaps spread out over a number of years, may be more important as a determinant of real wages than the general *level* of unemployment. This could reflect a strong segmentation or duality in labour markets but also the increase in the number of "unemployment pensioners" (see below), who are classified in official statistics as being unemployed, unlike in other countries. A decline in labour demand sheds a large part of the unemployed into "unemployment pension", but improving demand conditions do not reduce this type of unemployment. Hence, it tends to add to the unemployment rate over time but does not significantly increase pressure on unions to reduce their wage claims. If this is an accurate description of the labour market, the room for policy manœuvre is more restricted since the negative impact on wage inflation, which the current employment gap entails, will eventually diminish as the natural rate adjusts to actual unemployment levels.

Real labour cost gap and employment. Another way of measuring the labour market responsiveness is to compare the real labour cost growth with productivity developments – a change in the so-called real labour cost gap. If real labour costs do not adjust promptly to changes in productivity growth, the emergence of a gap may be seen as a sign of rigidity which partly explains an increase in unemployment. The real labour cost gap was increasing on trend to the mid-1970s, when the labour share of value added reached its peak and unemployment rose sharply. The adjustment to a more "normal" level thereafter was rather rapid, taking about two years, and since the beginning of the 1980s, real wage increases have followed developments of productivity (Diagram 11). The rapid narrowing of the gap can be partly explained in terms of the Phillips curve but, as noted above, the role of incomes policy based on adjustments of income taxes and social security contributions was also important.

The real labour cost gap adjustment took place also through productivity gains which reflected labour shedding due to cutbacks in unprofitable production and substitution of capital for labour. Diagram 12 shows how labour has been displaced by capital in the last fifteen years. In the early 1970s a widening of the real labour cost gap and negative real interest rates were associated with a very high and rising ratio of investment to value-added. Capital-labour ratios were increasing steeply, especially in capital-intensive industries (forestry, basic metals, energy). After the first oil shock, the investment ratio decreased for the rest of the decade, but the capital-labour ratio continued to rise due to a different set of forces. Profitability shrank markedly in 1975-77, but despite a strong shake-out of labour, the required wage adjustment was delayed, taking place as late as in 1977[34]. But marked changes in relative prices had made a part of capital stock obsolete, and led to cuts in unprofitable production. Between 1974 and 1978 the number of industrial enterprises decreased by 600 or by 4 per cent and manning was reduced by 8.2 per cent or 47 000 persons (see Annex I, Table 1). Labour shake-out in industry and commercial enterprises peaked in 1977 attaining 64 000 persons and raised the unemployment rate from 2.6 per cent in 1975 to 5.9 per cent. Higher unemployment (and probably also changed bargaining attitudes) was eventually felt in real wage developments, and a relatively moderate gain (1.9 per cent) during the cyclical upswing in 1978-80 went hand-in-hand with a slowdown in the growth of the capital-labour ratio. But the problem remains that although the gap has narrowed, the cost of labour relative both to capital and to labour abroad may remain too high.

Diagram 11. **The real labour cost gap**

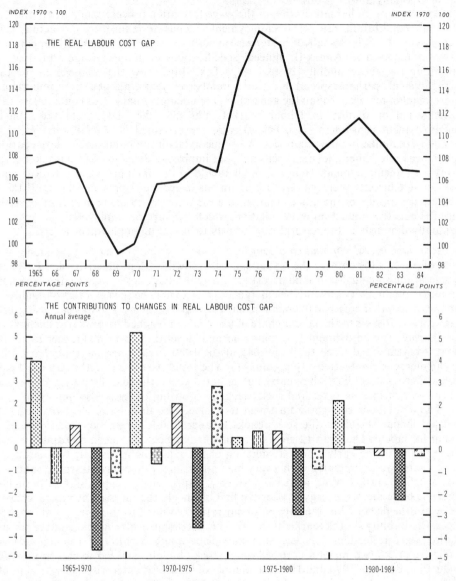

INDEX 1970 = 100   INDEX 1970 100

THE REAL LABOUR COST GAP

PERCENTAGE POINTS   PERCENTAGE POINTS

THE CONTRIBUTIONS TO CHANGES IN REAL LABOUR COST GAP
Annual average

1965-1970   1970-1975   1975-1980   1980-1984

▨ Real wage, net of employee-s social security contributions.

▨ Terms of trade.

▨ Tax wedge, defined as a change of $(1+t^E)/1-t^W)$ where t^E and t^W are employers' and workers' social security contribution rates.

▨ Productivity growth.

▨ Total change in real labour cost gap.

Source: OECD.

36

Diagram 12. **The capital-output and capital-labour ratio**
1970-1985

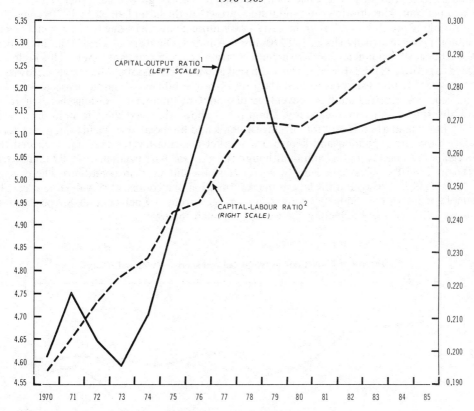

1. Gross fixed capital stock divided by total output, 1980 prices.
2. Net fixed capital stock at 1980 prices divided by total employment.
Source: OECD.

The adjustment process in Finland, as noted above, involved increasing capital-labour and capital-output ratios – i.e. a capital deepening process – in response to a delay in nominal wage adjustment and to more pessimistic demand expectations fuelled by the oil shocks, the severe domestic recession in 1975-77 and the international recession in the early 1980s. The relationship between investment and employment deteriorated sharply after 1975 and the share of machinery and equipment in total fixed capital formation increased markedly (see Annex I, Diagrams 2 and 3). The capacity utilisation rate decreased in 1976-78 to the lowest levels since the beginning of the 1960s. In the 1980s, utilisation rates have recovered towards "normal" levels, although a slack of some 2 to 3½ per cent has remained. At the same time the growth of labour supply has been unexpectedly rapid and has exceeded the growth of full capacity labour demand. If 1980 is considered as a full capacity year, the elimination of capacity slack would require the utilisation rate to be increased by some 2½ per cent, which would reduce the rate of unemployment by just 1 per cent to a little over 5 per cent. This points to the possibility of capital shortage as a factor behind high structural unemployment.

Net capital stock is estimated to have increased during the first half of the 1970s by more than 5 per cent annually, but, since then the annual average growth has fallen back to only about 3 per cent. The slowdown in capital stock growth in the latter half of the 1970s coincided with shrinking profitability, but in the early 1980s it must have been due to other factors since profitability has returned to its early 1970s level (Annex I, Diagram 4). Crucial in this respect is the tendency for financial assets to acquire a larger share in company assets. This is closely related to positive yield differentials between real and financial assets, which have narrowed in recent years. If interest rates exceed the rate of profitability and output expectations are depressed, cost cutting and improvement of company financial positions become more attractive than expansion of capacity. Diagram 12 shows that real short-term interest rates (which in Finland are relevant for new investments and financial asset yields since long-term interest rates are regulated and kept below market clearing levels) have not exceeded the average net rate of return on capital, although the gap was narrowing in 1975-77 and nearly closed in 1983-84. This may lead to a labour shake-out even in conditions where wage moderation is occurring and the labour market function in a comparatively flexible way. The unemployment rate in industry rose in just a year from 6.5 per cent to 8.2 per cent in January 1986, possibly reflecting the working of such forces.

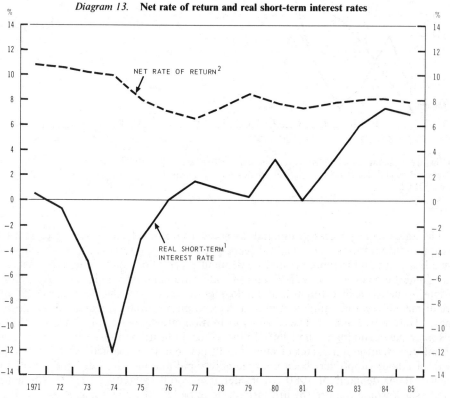

Diagram 13.   **Net rate of return and real short-term interest rates**

1. Call money rate minus per cent change in GDP deflator.
2. Operating surplus as per cent of net fixed capital stock, total industries.
Source: OECD.

Labour market slack: structural features

There is some evidence that structural changes in the labour market have played a role in maintaining unemployment at high levels through the 1980s. The relation between capacity utilisation and employment – the so-called Okun curve – appears to have shifted upwards in the second half of the 1970s. Thus, while in the mid-1970s a capacity utilisation rate of

Diagram 14. **The Okun curve in Finland and in Europe**

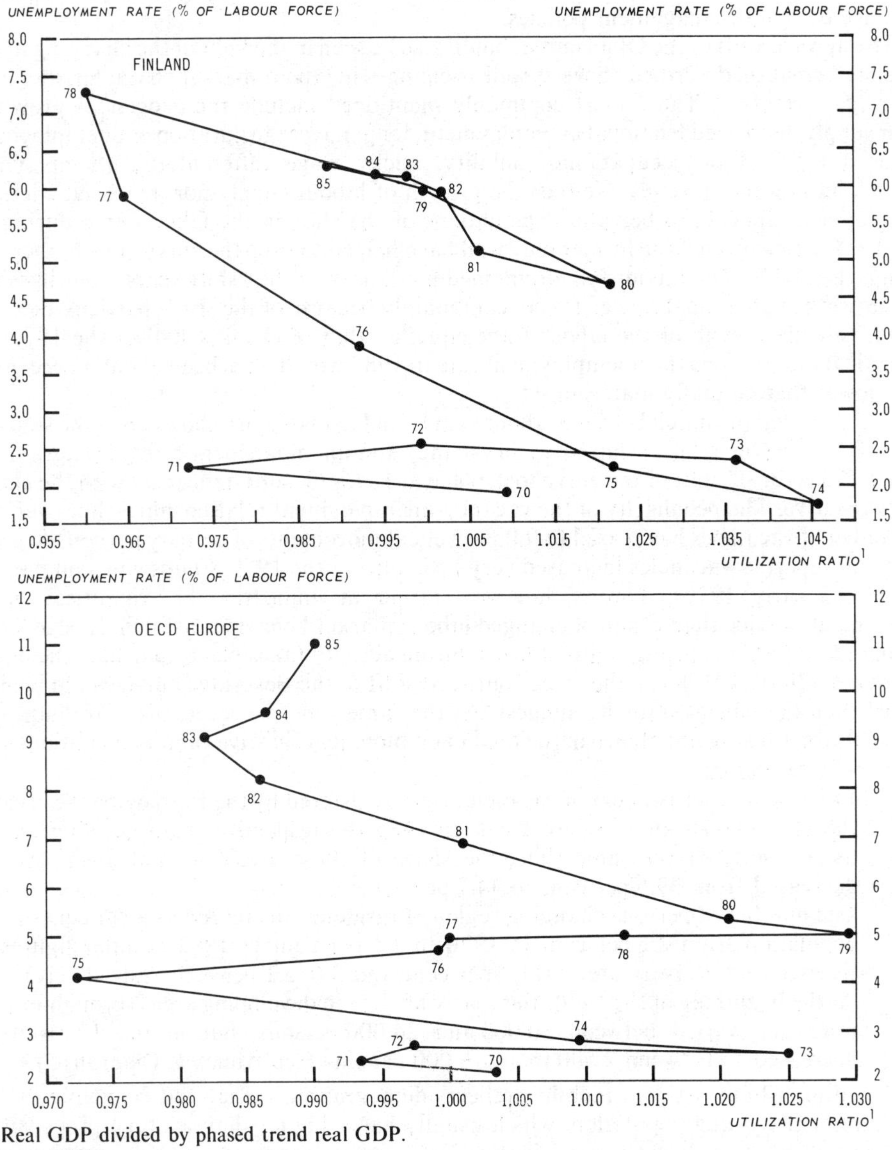

UNEMPLOYMENT RATE (% OF LABOUR FORCE)   UNEMPLOYMENT RATE (% OF LABOUR FORCE)

1. Real GDP divided by phased trend real GDP.
Source: OECD.

39

approximately 95 per cent was associated with an unemployment rate of about 2 per cent, in the 1980s the unemployment rate increased to about 6 per cent at the same level of capacity utilisation. The shift in the Okun curve has, however, been less pronounced in Finland than elsewhere in Europe, where the unemployment rate at a high level of capacity use has increased from about 3 per cent in the early 1970s to 10 to 11 per cent in the 1980s (Diagram 14). This partly reflects differences in the speed of real wage adjustment. As mentioned above, real wage growth relative to productivity growth began to decelerate in Finland already after the first oil shock, whereas in Europe the real wage moderation generally began only after the second oil shock with high and rising unemployment and restrictive demand-management policies.

The upward shift of the Okun curve should also be seen in the light of the changing nature of capital formation described above as well as changes in labour market characteristics other than wage formation. Those most commonly mentioned include the exogenous growth of labour supply, increased frictional unemployment, longer average duration of unemployment, decreased regional or occupational mobility, sticky wage differentials, unemployment benefits and minimum wages. Neither the growth of labour supply nor increased frictional unemployment appears to be valid explanations of the shift in the Okun curve during the 1976-1978 period, even if the former may well have helped to keep the curve at its higher level through the 1980s. The labour force remained stationary in the "shift years", but has since been growing at an annual rate of 1½ per cent mainly because of the rising participation rate. Indeed, had the growth of the labour force equalled that of the first half of the 1970s, on mechanical calculations the unemployment rate in 1985 would have been about 3 percentage points lower than actually materialised.

The growing mismatch between labour supply and demand also shows up in the so-called Beveridge curve (the relationship between vacancy and unemployment rates) (Diagram 15). Again a "structural" shift of the curve took place in 1976-78, simultaneously with the shift in the Okun curve. The peculiarity of the vacancy-unemployment relationship is, however, that the number of vacancies has ceased to follow cyclical movements of activity in the 1980s. The number of reported vacancies increased very little during the 1979-80 upswing compared to that of the early 1970s. This is, however, rather an indication of "rigidities" in the Employment Service than a sign of changed labour market behaviour as such. It is generally considered that an increasing share of firms' hiring activity takes place "outside" the official Employment Service[35]. Thus, the "true" outward shift of the Beveridge curve would be more marked than the official statistics suggest. At the same time, however, there are indicators that point to a growing imbalance in regional unemployment/job availability conditions since the 1976-78 recession:

- In 1978 some 61 per cent of vacancies were registered by the Employment Service in the Helsinki-Turku-Tampere areas. In 1985 the respective share had increased to 64 per cent. At the same time, the share of these areas in total unemployment decreased from 39.5 per cent to 34.7 per cent.
- The number of persons changing region of residence decreased as a per cent of total population from 2.5 per cent in 1970 to 1.5 per cent in 1982 (similar figures for Sweden and Norway are 2.4/1.7 per cent and 3.0/2.1 per cent respectively).
- At the beginning of the 1970s the yearly net loss in developing areas through internal migration varied between 10 000 and 24 000 persons, but in the 1980s it has decreased to between 2 500 to and 6 000 persons (see Annex I, Diagram 5).

The diminishing regional mobility reflects demographic, social and economic factors. The share of the young population, which usually has a higher-than-average propensity to move, has decreased. Female participation rates have increased, making moving more

Diagram 15. **The Beveridge curve**

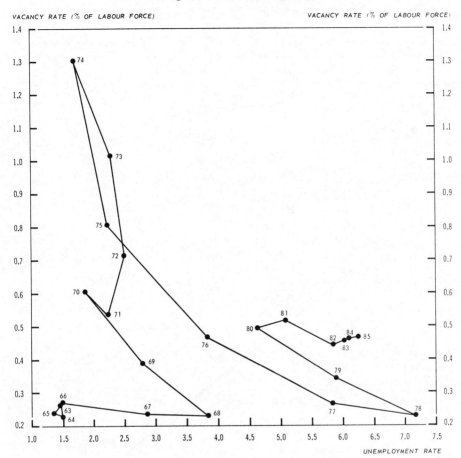

VACANCY RATE (% OF LABOUR FORCE)

UNEMPLOYMENT RATE

Source: OECD Secretariat.

dependent on job availability for both spouses. Owner-occupied housing has become more widespread and housing availability is often lacking in areas where the demand for labour is strongest. At the same time, unemployment benefits and high marginal tax rates may have been acting as disincentives to move. Wage-earners may have little or no financial incentive to take jobs even if they are available, relying on unemployment and other social welfare benefits as well as on certain income tax free earnings (Northern Finland) and earnings in the "hidden" economy for income maintenance. A related phenomenon is the "unemployment pension". Older unemployed are allowed to retire on "unemployment pension" after 200 days of unemployment. The age limit was temporarily reduced from 60 to 55 years between 1980 and 1986. The number of such pensioners has since 1980 increased rapidly, attaining in 1985 some 38 000 persons, or about 1½ per cent of the labour force according to the Labour Survey[36]. Since the inclusion of unemployment pensioners in official unemployment statistics, the unemployment rate has become strongly biased upwards. As noted, this is one of the most straightforward explanations of the shift in the Okun curve.

41

Diagram 16. **Real wage rigidity and wage differentials**

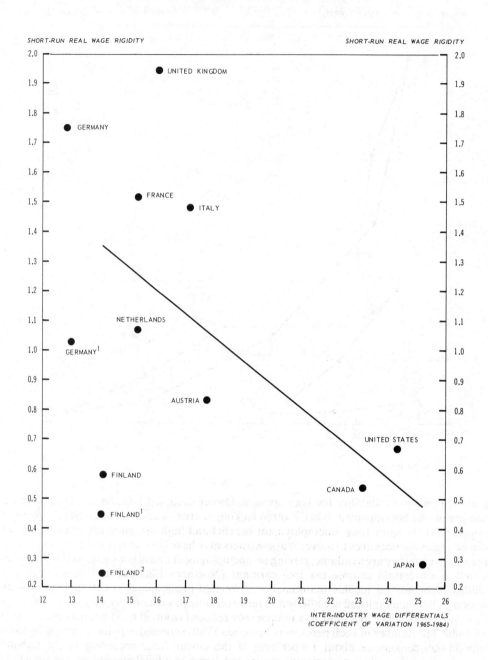

1. Productivity as an additional explanatory variable.
2. Hysteresis specification of Phillips curve.
Source: OECD.

Occupational matching problems have added to increased structural unemployment[37]. A mismatch index[38] increased markedly between 1975 and 1978. Employment grew strongly in the service sector, while the major part of rising unemployment was due to labour shedding in industry and construction. A growing number of young, often better trained, entrants to the labour market "displaced" older persons, when labour demand increased in the 1979-80 upswing and the youth unemployment rate fell from 13 to 10 per cent. Consequently the average duration of unemployment rose continually over this period. While the decrease in occupational mobility is apparently much the result of a slowdown of economic growth it is also connected with demographic changes. The findings in other countries show that occupational mobility declines strongly with age and this may well be the major factor at work in Finland. Moreover, education policy also plays a role. Education programmes and decisions concerning the capacity in specific branches of medium and higher education are based on long-term planning, but rapidly changing needs of the economy are not easily translated into such programmes. For young people, however, the correspondence between training and jobs may be judged as still rather good in Finland, as youth unemployment has remained relatively low by international standards. For adults having lost their jobs as a result of structural changes in the economy, the problem appears to be more severe as apparent in the increasing length of unemployment spells for higher age groups.

Job tenure and labour turnover serve also as partial yardsticks of labour market functioning. The shorter the job tenure and the higher the labour turnover, the more flexible would the labour market be to adjust to changing structural needs. The average completed job tenure in Finland was 16½ years in 1983, whereas it ranged from 13 years in Australia to 23 years in Japan. The share of short-term job spells (under one year) decreased from 24 to 16 per cent between 1973 and 1983, and simultaneously the share of more than ten-year employment duration increased from 23 to 32 per cent, being, however, lower than most European countries' experience in the late 1970s. The complementary measure, the rate of labour turnover in firms, declined after OPEC I with the general tendency towards lower job mobility. At the beginning of the 1980s, however, Finland compares well with the highest job mobility country, the United States, with turnover rates of 36 to 40 respectively. There is, however, no simple relationship between mobility rates and the allocative efficiency of the labour market. For instance, the United States and Japan, the two countries often quoted for their high degree of labour market "flexibility", have quite different job mobility patterns. However, a certain degree of job mobility is always needed in an economy when it adjusts to external shocks and/or structural changes. The decline in job mobility in Finland owes much to the factors also responsible for declines in regional and occupational mobility. However, it may be taken as a sign of increasing labour market duality or segmentation, if the short-term job tenure is concentrated on the same group of workers.

Lower mobility of workers is often related to low dispersion of wages among branches and regions. The wage dispersion in the economy as a whole has been decreasing in Finland since the mid-1960s in common with the experience of most OECD European countries (see Annex I, Diagram 6). In industry, however, dispersion has widened in the last 25 years, although the differentials are not much wider than in many European countries (but narrower than in the United States and Japan). Plotting wage differentials in industry against measures of real wage rigidity, reveals a clear negative relationship internationally, i.e. narrow differentials are generally associated with inflexible real wages and vice versa (Diagram 16). Wage differentials are often seen to be related to changes in the rate of inflation and changing demand pressures. In countries where real wages are flexible (United States and Japan), pay differentials tend to widen with rising inflation, whereas if the real wages are rigid the pay differentials will tend to narrow (France and Italy). However in Finland widening differentials mirror diverging inter-industry productivity developments (which seep into wages through wagedrift) rather than interaction between inflation and wage differentials[39]. The widening of wage differentials in industry may also be a reflection of the labour market segmentation referred to above. In the 1960s, there were only few firms at the extreme ends of the wage distribution, while in the subsequent decade the distribution resembled more a normal bell shape. In the last few years there has been a much stronger polarisation of firms belonging either to "low pay" or "high pay" groups[40]. Non-wage labour cost, replacement ratios and minimum wages all appear to be unimportant in explaining Finnish wage differentials[41].

As noted in several places in the discussion above, there is evidence that the Finnish labour market has important characteristics of duality:

- The econometric work pointed to segmentation of labour markets as did large regional differences in the unemployment rate[42] and in the unemployment-vacancy relationship;
- The number of long-duration unemployed[43] have created dualistic features also among the unemployed;
- Increased duality was also observed when wage differentials are considered with industries concentrating in "low pay" and "high pay" groups, probably demanding rather different skill qualifications.

This phenomenon can even be observed in unemployment benefits and employment service systems. Two separate unemployment benefit schemes are in operation: a general unemployment insurance where benefits are lower and the "customers" typically are low-skilled, short-time "jobbers" and consequently frequently unemployed; and an earnings-dependent system, which typically covers union members with a comparatively better job history. As noted above, the hiring practice of firms also takes place through two channels; the official Employment Service with a rapidly-declining "market share" and the direct hiring through press, private agencies and other informal channels. The labour market is so to speak divided into two sectors, where, on the one hand, there exists a group of well-paid core workers with good working conditions, long duration of employment and with little competition from the "outside" labour market. In the secondary sector pay is low, durations of employment usually short and jobs are under permanent competition on the labour market. A rough estimate of the number of workers belonging to this secondary category in 1980 can be made from the number of short-duration employees. The Finnish Employment Service Offices have patronised half a million job applicants annually, most of whom belong to the secondary sector[44].

IV. CONCLUSIONS

Since the second oil shock the growth of output and employment in Finland has been well above the European average and this has taken place without creating balance of payments problems. The excellent growth performance reflected an earlier adjustment of the Finnish economy to the first oil shock than in other European countries, an adjustment which showed up in growth rates below the European average in the second half of the 1970s accompanied by labour-shedding which peaked in 1977. Finland has also benefited from special structural features. The importance of bilateral trade with the Soviet Union, with oil being the main import item, helped sustain the expansion of exports when demand in Western markets suffered from the aftermath of the second oil shock. Moreover, the strong dollar also increased exports to the Soviet Union because the ruble has tended to follow the dollar and boosted the competitiveness of paper, pulp and forestry products industries, the diminishing but still important part of Finnish exports, vis-à-vis North American producers.

A remarkable aspect of economic achievements in the 1980s is the stability of annual growth rates which deviated little from 3 per cent except in 1981. Policy played an important role in generating stability. There have been marked changes in the policy approach in Finland since the late 1970s. Fiscal policy, by attempting to balance the budget position each year, had resulted in a procyclical fiscal stance, amplifying fluctuations in activity. Following the relaxation of the budget balancing requirement, fiscal policy has been operated in a countercyclical fashion. Moreover, the authorities' attitude towards maintaining the external value of the markka has become more determined. Changes in the bargaining behaviour and active use of tax-based incomes policy have moderated domestic wage-cost pressure and contributed to stabilising the exchange rate. Even so, wage pressure has remained higher than in competitor countries and monetary policy has had to remain tight. With the greater internationalisation of the financial markets in recent years differentials between domestic and foreign interest rates have become an important consideration of monetary policy. Financial markets have become more exposed to sporadic speculative pressures. Deregulation has added to the greater sensitivity of domestic financial markets to movements in international interest rates which, though declining, have remained high. Net results have been sharply higher domestic interest rates, especially in real terms, although since the late 1970s positive real interest rates have been considered desirable from the point of view of improving the efficiency of capital investment.

Prospects for the immediate future are clouded by the unwinding of the exceptional influences which favoured Finland in recent years. Lower oil prices strongly affect trade with the Soviet Union, although the flexibility in financing arrangements can alleviate the problem somewhat. Thus, together with the lagged impact of worsening price competitiveness, export volumes are expected to remain flat this year and next. The main source of buoyancy is consumption, both private and public, reflecting the terms-of-trade gains, new wage settlements and adjustments of the tax brackets, the effect of the latter being only partly offset by the shifting of energy taxation from business to households. Thus, the Secretariat's forecasts are that in 1986 and 1987, for the first time since 1978, real GDP growth in Finland may lag behind the average of OECD Europe. The unemployment rate is projected to edge up towards 7 per cent in 1987. Consumer price inflation, however, may approach rates prevailing in main competitor countries. The current external deficit will probably remain small as the adverse volume effects are neutralised by the terms-of-trade gains.

As noted above, bilateral trade with the Soviet Union has acted as a balancing item for firms which have suffered from the weakness of Western markets and intensified competitive pressure which in certain industries has been due to heavy subsidisation by the main competitor countries. In addition, the strong dollar had until recently shielded key sectors from North American competition. The unwinding of the special external factors is likely to be increasing adjustment pressure in the years to come, exacerbated by the difficulty in switching from Eastern to Western markets in the short run. Such adjustment difficulties are reflected in the projected weakness of exports in the near future. However, the adaptability of Finnish industry would appear to remain good in view of little direct government subsidisation of private enterprises outside agriculture. Recent merger activities and increased specialisation in certain branches suggest that some adjustments are already under way.

Looking beyond the next eighteen months, certain underlying developments are disquieting. Although wage growth has moderated somewhat in Finland, the moderation has not been sufficient in relation to what has happened in the main competitor countries so that cost competitiveness has been deteriorating. More generally, incentives to strive for lower inflation and hence better price competitiveness have been weakened by the increasing importance of the sheltered sector in wage negotiations and the maintenance of price regulation in certain key areas. However, the deterioration in competitiveness has been offset to some extent by the cost-reducing effect of the energy tax package and by corporate tax reform, and measures have been announced recently to reduce official price control and limit restrictive business practices. Nevertheless, lower spring 1986 settlements which cover two years would have reduced the costs of the exchange rate maintenance by allowing lower unemployment and better external balance than are being projected. One obvious consequence of deteriorating competitiveness is that the pursuit of the stable exchange rate policy will require continuing high interest rates in order to attract sufficient net capital inflows to finance the current external deficit. Such a requirement appears likely to be augmented by a structural deterioration in the invisibles account and the eventual disappearance of the terms-of-trade gains.

Influenced by the favourable development of household real disposable income and probably also by high real interest rates, the composition of demand has changed in favour of consumption and this tendency is projected to continue. Such a demand configuration does not appear to be appropriate from the point of view of sustaining economic growth over the medium term. However, this assessment should be qualified by the fact that high real interest rates may have improved the quality of fixed investment and that the importance of outlays on intangible assets has been increasing.

The slower growth of capital stock relative to the 1970s has resulted not only from weaker investment activities but also from increased scrapping of obsolete capital assets. This, combined with the increasingly labour-saving nature of new investments, has been partly responsible for the observed increase in the unemployment rate relative to the slack of capacity use – the so-called Okun curve which is a broad indicator of the mismatch between demand and supply of labour. As discussed in Part III such a mismatch has apparently been increased by the rapid growth in the number of unemployed pensioners as well as by reduced labour mobility both across regions and occupations. The degree of segmentation in the labour market appears to have risen, leading to a dualistic structure in broad terms. This would limit the scope for reducing unemployment by means of higher aggregate demand without exacerbating domestic inflationary pressures.

In Finland, as in other countries, the inflation/unemployment trade-off is a central policy issue. The analysis presented in Part III of the present Survey suggests that in recent years the actual unemployment rate has remained above the rate below which inflation tends to accelerate – the so-called NAIRU – though the measurement is necessarily subject to certain margins of error. The Secretariat's projection suggests that this gap will widen in the next eighteen months or so. However, much uncertainty attaches to the extent to which this will be reflected in cost and price trends. Given the increased segmentation of the labour market, it is possible that the NAIRU is indeed higher than estimated. The settlements just concluded point to this possibility. Stronger efforts designed to make the labour market more flexible, including continuous retraining of manpower whether employed or not, would thus merit serious consideration, all the more so since further wage moderation is so important in reducing the cost of maintaining the exchange rate of the markka.

Empirical analyses indicate that wages are rather flexible compared with most other OECD countries. So far, however, a significant part of wage moderation has been brought about by tax concessions of various forms. This, and more importantly, the rapid rise in public expenditure, was accompanied by an increase in the public debt-to-GDP ratio. While this ratio has stabilised as a ratio of GDP at a level which is still low by international comparison, the experience in many OECD countries suggests that it is difficult to keep the growth of debt under control when real interest rates are high. The problem arises in part from the fact that it is often difficult to distinguish cyclical weakening in activity from the trend slowdown in growth so that what was meant to be a countercyclical, temporary increase in the budget deficit has tended to become permanent. It is also more difficult politically to cut public expenditure than to increase it. A similar point applies also to the tax-based incomes policy in that tax concessions appear to have become *sine qua non* of wage settlements. This is a potentially dangerous process through which the responsibility of social partners in agreeing on wages is diluted. The weakening of discipline in wage negotiations will not be compatible with the stable exchange rate policy over the longer haul.

In sum, Finland has been able to tide over the difficult period after the second oil shock better than many other OECD countries. The excellent performance in the last five years or so has been made possible by a more rapid adjustment to the first oil shock than generally elsewhere in Europe. The change in policy orientation with more flexible fiscal policy and greater determination to pursue the policy of a stable exchange rate since the late 1970s has played a significant role in attenuating fluctuations in activity, and the importance of bilateral trade with the Soviet Union as well as the strong dollar have contributed to sustaining demand. The policy approach adopted, while successful in its own right, has had some negative side effects which have probably been inevitable. Symptomatic of these are the reduced share of investment in GDP, high levels of real interest rates, gradual erosion of cost competitiveness and the increase in public debt, all of which are inter-related. The major source of difficulty, though not yet serious, is persistently high wage cost pressure which, through its negative effect on international competitiveness, has made it necessary to maintain higher interest rates than abroad in order to keep the stable nominal exchange rate and has contributed to the weakened investment trends. The Government's attempt to bring down wage claims through tax concessions was partly responsible for the increase in public debt. Empirical studies show that wages are relatively more flexible in Finland than in most other OECD countries and that a tax-based incomes policy partly accounts for such flexibility. There are also signs that labour markets have become more segmented and hence any given level of unemployment would represent tighter labour market conditions than before. It is for these reasons that stepped-up policy efforts to improve the functioning of the labour market would be worthwhile. More generally, policymakers are faced with the challenge of overcoming those side effects of policy mentioned above.

NOTES AND REFERENCES

1. The share of exports to the Soviet Union grew from about 14 per cent of total exports in the mid-1970s to a peak of 25 per cent in 1981/82. Since then the share has fallen back to around 20 per cent. From 1981 to 1985 the volume of exports to Eastern markets increased by 27 per cent, but to the West by only 13 per cent. About 80 per cent of imports from the Soviet Union is energy.

2. The other countries are the United States, Canada, Iceland, Norway and Sweden.

3. Within the public sector it is notably in local governments where employment has expanded in conjunction with various social reforms (particularly in health).

4. In contrast to many other OECD countries, growth of part-time employment has only had a relatively minor influence on the evolution of overall employment trends in the 1980s. In the ten years from 1973, part-time employment as a proportion of total employment increased from 6.7 per cent to 8.7 per cent, though with an appreciable involuntary element.

5. Rising participation rates account for over half of the labour force increase since 1980.

6. Notably the social security sector accounts for most of the long-run deterioration of the general government financial balance as a consequence of a number of comprehensive welfare and health reforms.

7. The somewhat low coefficient for imported inflation reflects the high import content of exports and the large share of raw materials in total imports, as well as the fact that part of the import price effects is captured by the food price variable.

8. For more details, see OECD Survey of Finland, December 1983, p.15.

9. Agricultural prices are set so as to compensate for past cost increases as measured by the input price indices. In general, the increase in farm incomes is closely linked to wage settlements in other sectors.

10. The recent stumpage price settlement is a departure from past practice. For the first time in the post-war period, nominal prices were lowered, reflecting the world-wide downward pressure on raw material prices.

11. The contribution of private and public consumption to the growth of real GDP was about two-thirds in the 1982-85 period.

12. Submission from the Bank of Finland.

13. See E. Horwitz, *Export competitiveness among the Nordic countries,* unpublished memo, 27th March 1986.

14. The price of oil imported from the Soviet Union follows that of North Sea oil with a relatively short time lag.

15. There is a formal "buffer" limit in the clearing account of about Mk 2 billion but experience suggests that the "room for manœuvre" is considerably larger due to special credit arrangements, removal of clearing account limits, prepayments, etc.

16. The June investment survey of the Bank of Finland reports some 8 per cent increase in manufacturing real investment. Investment activity was, however, mainly concentrated in state-owned companies, whereas the volume of private companies' investment increased by only 3 per cent in 1985.

17. In 1986, a 5 per cent decline is expected, followed by a 20 per cent reduction in 1987. If the assumed oil price fall is fully taken into account, export volumes should be lower by some 38 per cent cumulatively.

18. The labour force is projected to grow during the 1986-90 period by 42 thousand persons, compared with 150 thousand during the 1980-85 period.

19. See e.g. Dahmen, E: *Ekonomi i omvandling,* Finlands Bank C:7, 1984; H. Halttunen and S. Korkman: External Shocks and Adjustment Policies in Finland, 1973-80 in De Cecco (ed.): *International Economic Adjustment,* Basil Blackwell, Oxford 1983 and J. Akerholm and J. Pekkarinen, Den finländska finanspolitiken- efterbliven och förutseende, *Ekonomisk Debatt 8, 1983.*

20. Between 1960 and 1980 the ratio of public sector outlays to GDP rose from 26.6 per cent to 37.2 per cent. In Sweden and Denmark, for example, the ratios rose from 31.1 per cent to 62.1 per cent, and from 24.8 per cent to 56.2 per cent respectively.

21. See OECD Survey of Finland, June 1985, Part III.

22. For a comprehensive review of the developments of financial markets in recent years and its implication for the monetary control framework see OECD Survey of Finland, May 1985, Part III.

23. Intervention in the forward market amounted at the end of 1984 to some Mk 20 billion, while net foreign reserves increased by Mk 9¾ billion.

24. These sales, stimulated by a combination of high yields, a favourable tax treatment and the stability of the exchange rate, developed as follows: 1983: Mk 0.2 billion; 1984: Mk 1.1 billion; and 1985 (first half-year): Mk 4.5 billion.

25. The diversification abroad of Finnish firms has been considerable in terms of direct investments. From a mere Mk 0.4 billion in 1980, the purchase of net equity capital abroad rose to Mk 2.1 billion in 1984, but fell back last year to Mk 1.8 billion.

26. Other OECD Member countries which have adopted a currency basket peg are New Zealand (1973 to 1984), Australia (1974 to 1983), Norway (since 1977) and Sweden (since 1977). See also OECD: *Exchange Rate Management and the Conduct of Monetary Policy,* OECD, Paris 1985, for the experiences of selected OECD Member countries.

27. Whereas the average deterioration of the terms of trade in the OECD area was some 10 per cent in 1974, Finland's terms of trade worsened only slightly and improved in 1975, owing to favourable movements in international prices of paper, pulp and timber.

28. The depreciation was prompted by the strength of the dollar, which was not fully offset by an appreciation of the markka vis-à-vis other currencies, because of the different weight attached to each currency.

29. See D.Coe, "Nominal wages, the NAIRU and Wage Flexibility", in *OECD Economic Studies,* No.5, Autumn 1985. The semi-elasticity of nominal wages with respect to a 1 percentage point increase in the unemployment rate varies between – 0.17 (the United Kingdom) and – 3.31 (Japan). The elasticity for Finland is estimated in two versions to be – 0.49 and – 0.52 slightly less than Austria and higher than other European countries.

30. The estimation methods used are regression-based transformations of aggregate unemployment rate (Kanniainen-Lilleberg, Santamäki); of Phillips curve estimates (Halttunen, Paunio-Suvanto, Koskela-Wiren, Pehkonen, Tarkka, Secretariat); or estimates of unemployment rate equations (Eriksson). See T. Eriksson: *Some Investigations into Finnish Unemployment Dynmamics, Abo 1985* and M. Ingberg, *Has the Functioning of the Finnish Labour Market Worsened?,* unpublished memo, 30th January 1986.

31. The 1977/78 settlements marked a new approach in incomes policies, with the Government becoming more heavily involved and using a wider spectrum of instruments (tax scale adjustments, child allowances, day-care expenditures) to reduce nominal wage claims.

32. Such an indicator is derived from the Phillips-curve relationship as a ratio of two elasticities, i.e. the short-run elasticity of nominal wages with respect to consumer prices and the semi-elasticity of nominal wages with respect to the unemployment rate. The lower the value of this ratio the more flexible real wages are.

33. See Coe, *op.cit.*

34. Indeed, growth of real wages in 1974-75 was cumulatively 5½ per cent, while in 1977 the real wage level was reduced by 1.5 per cent.

35. Presently, only a fourth of all vacancies is reported to the Ministry of Labour, whose "market share" has diminished from 42 per cent in 1972 to 24 per cent in 1985, mainly because of employers' increased qualification demands, higher share of white collar workers who traditionally go through different recruiting channels and a decreased share of seasonal work.

36. Ministry of Labour Statistics show the number of unemployed pensioners at 54 000, but of these all are not classified as "unemployed" in official unemployment statistics.

37. See Eriksson, *op.cit.*

38. The formula proposed by Nickell (1982) is calculated as $H = \sqrt{\Sigma u_i\, v_i}$ where $u_i = U_i/U$ and $v_i = V_i/V$ and U is the number of unemployed, V = number of registered vacancies. The sub-index denotes the occupation in question (see Annex I, Table 2).

39. A preliminary econometric study of the Economic Planning Centre in Finland reports significant links between productivity differentials and wage dispersion in industry; an increase of 1 percentage point in productivity differential gives rise to an increase in wage differentials by 0.13 percentage points.

40. Preliminary results from a wage differential study of the Economic Planning Centre.

41. Non-wage labour costs in Finland are not to any meaningful extent connected with ceiling provisions which exist in most European countries. The replacement ratios of unemployment benefits have in the past been well under the European level, and they are still comparatively moderate, although the unemployment benefit system was renewed in 1985 and the replacement ratios were raised (Annex I, Table 3). Research on Finnish data lends no support to the role of minimum wages in explaining youth unemployment. The aggregate demand effects outweigh the labour supply effect, which seems to be the general conclusion also in other countries. The significance of minimum wages for female or low-skilled workers' unemployment is obviously negligible because the level of minimum wage has remained too low to have any push effect on wages in general.

42. For regional unemployment rates, see Annex I, Table 4.

43. According to official statistics the share of long-term unemployment is low by international standards (14.4 per cent in 1984). However, analytically the unemployment pensioners form a part of long-term unemployment even though they are not so classified in official statistics. Including these, the share would increase to some 30 per cent, close to the average European level.

44. See N. Sääski, *Labour market functioning,* Labour Reports, 1981.

Annex I

SUPPLEMENTARY TABLES AND DIAGRAMS

Table AI.1.   **Industrial and commercial enterprises**

	Industrial		Commercial	
	Number of firms	Personnel	Number of firms	Personnel
1974	15 212	575 313	28 842	271 336
1976	14 933	571 424	27 716	265 870
1978	14 604	528 362	28 708	254 325
1980	16 239	572 093	30 438	260 665

Source: Statistical Yearbook of Finland.

Table AI.2.   **Occupational mismatch index**

1970	0.940	1978	0.900
1971	0.930	1979	0.960
1972	0.925	1980	0.930
1973	0.935	1981	0.930
1974	0.950	1982	0.915
1975	0.900	1983	0.910
1976	0.905	1984	0.885
1977	0.900		

Source: Eriksson T., *op. cit.*

Table A1.3. **Replacement ratios**[1]

Per cent

	Civil servants	Skilled industrial workers	Young unemployed (18 years)
Unemployed for one year			
Finland[2]	48	50	43
Sweden	58	81	92
Norway	55	67	68
Denmark	46	66	90
Unemployed for three months			
Finland[2]	88	88	85
Sweden	89	94	96
Norway	88	91	91
Denmark	87	92	97

1. After-tax income of an unemployed person as per cent of yearly after-tax income of an employed person.
2. Single worker.
Source: Nordiska Rådet, *Arbejdsloshedens omkostninger i Norden*, Slutrapport, NU 1985:2.

Table A1.4. **Regional unemployment rates**

Per cent

	1976	1980	1984
Helsinki	2.2	2.8	2.6
Turku	3.4	3.4	5.3
Tampere	3.9	4.8	7.4
Kouvola	3.6	4.7	7.0
Mikkeli	5.7	6.3	6.8
Vaasa	3.6	3.1	5.4
Jyväskylä	5.6	5.1	7.6
Kuupio	6.2	5.6	8.2
Joensuu	6.1	7.1	9.0
Kajaani	8.8	10.5	12.7
Oulu	4.5	9.9	11.9
Whole country	3.9	4.7	6.2

Source: Ministry of Labour.

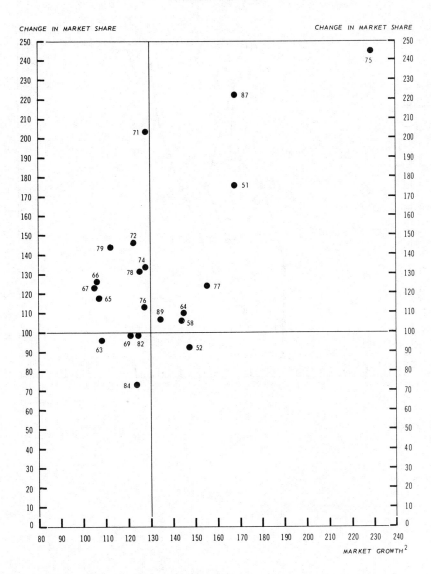

Diagram A1.1 **Market shares and market growth for manufacturing in Finland, 1978-1984**

Index 1978 = 100[1]

1. Industrial branches according to SITC classification.
2. Constant market shares adjusted.
Source: E. Horwitz, *op.cit.*

53

Diagram AI.2 **Investment and employment**

Index 1980 = 100

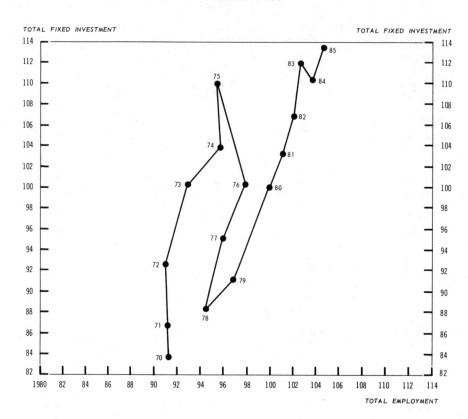

Source: **OECD.**

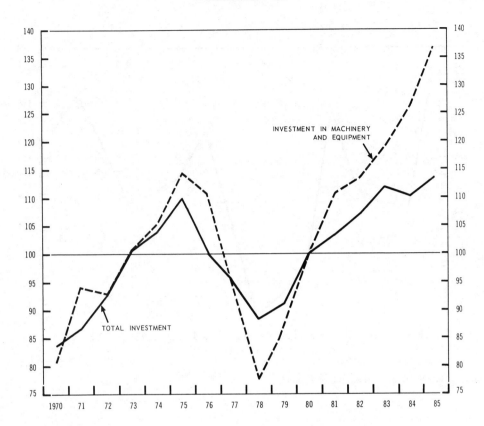

Diagram AI.3 **Investment in machinery and equipment (1980 prices)**
Index 1980 = 100

Source: OECD.

Diagram AI.4 Profitability in manufacturing
Ratio of gross operating surplus to gross capital stock

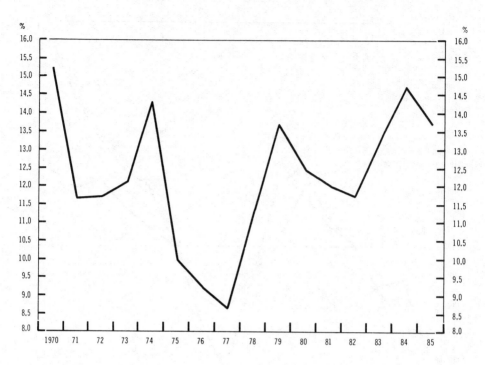

Source: Submission from the Bank of Finland.

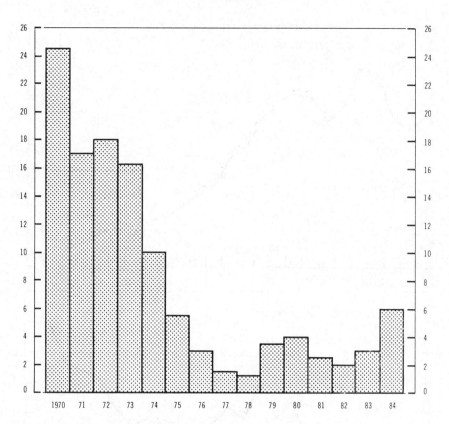

Source: Ministry of Labour.

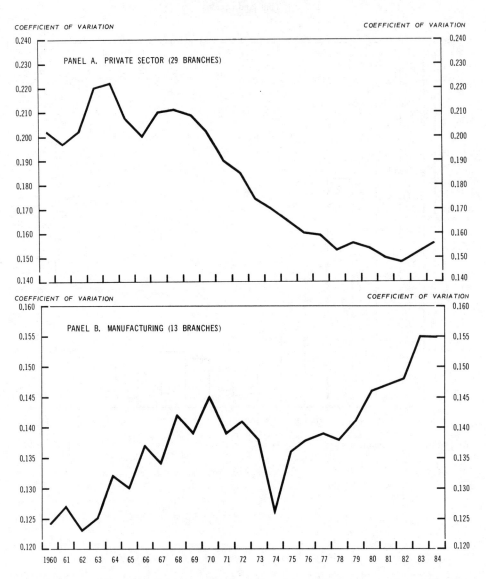

1. Measured by the sample coefficient of variation defined as the standard deviation divided by the mean.
Source: Submission from the Economic Planning Centre.

Annex II

WAGE AND PRICE EQUATIONS

The wage equation

The econometric analysis of Finnish labour market flexibility which underlies Part III of the main text, assumes that nominal wage growth reflects labour markets disequilibrium. In the long run, market forces move the labour market to equilibrium at the natural rate of unemployment (the rate compatible with the steady state growth of productivity and past or expected inflation). The dynamic adjustment process of nominal wages is described by an expectations augmented Phillips curve, which relates the rate of change of wages *(w)* to expected consumer price inflation *(pe)*, the unemployment rate *(u)* and a vector of other relevant variables (X)[1].

(1) $\quad w_t = a0 + a1.pe_t - a2.u_t + a3.X_t$

The labour market disequilibrium variable is the official unemployment rate, and the equilibrium components are the constant (which implicitly incorporates a constant natural rate of unemployment) and inflation term. Relevant variables included in X might reflect alternative theories of wage formation or country specific influences on nominal wage growth. From estimates of parameter values in the above equation (or different specifications of it) specific measures of labour markets flexibility can be derived as well as giving information about the prospects for short and long-run inflation developments.

The price equation and NAIRU

When inflation is also considered as endogenous phenomenon, it is possible to compute the level of unemployment rate which is consistent with stable inflation – the NAIRU. The approach adopted has been to combine the augmented Phillips curve (equation 1) with a cost mark-up price relationship (equation 2) in order to compute the NAIRU. In the price equation

(2) $\quad p_t = b0 + b1 \Sigma L1_i (w + s - q)_{t-i} + b2 \Sigma L2ipm_{t-1} + b3.Z_t$

p is the rate of change of prices, s is the rate of change of one plus the effective tax rate on employer's social security contributions, q is trend productivity growth, pm is the rate of change of import prices and Z is a vector of other relevant variables. The $L1_i$ and $L2_i$ are lag distributions, which sum to unity. The coefficients of relevant cost variables (*w + s, pm*, Z) should sum up to unity and the coefficients of wage and productivity variables should be equal and of opposite sign. By assuming that expectations are realised (*p = pe* for all *t*) the reduced form wage equation from the wage-price block can be solved by inserting equation (2) into (1). Thus, the equation for the NAIRU (U) is:

(3) $\quad U = (1/a2)[(a0 + a1.b0) - (1 - a1.b1) w + a1.b1 (s - q) + a1.b2.pm + a1.b3.Z + a3.X]$

If it is further assumed, that nominal wage growth eventually adjusts to price inflation, i.e. $a1 = 1$ and that in the case of a small open economy the domestic costs and import prices change at the same rate over the longer run, i.e. $w = pm$, assuming that $b2 = 1-b1$ equation (3) reduces to:

(4) $\quad U = [a0 + b0 + b1 (s - q) + b3.Z + a3X]/a2$

With these assumptions there is no relationship between wage inflation and employment and hence the long run Phillips curve is vertical. The NAIRU for Finland is, however, calculated from equation (3) using the parameter values of wage and price equations.

The data

The semi-annual changes in nominal wages are calculated for the private sector as national accounts wages and salaries per dependent employeee. The inflation variable is the implicit private consumption deflator. The unemployment rate is based on official unemployment statistics of the Statistical Central Office. Productivity is defined as real GDP divided by total employment. The employers' social security contribution rate variable includes the statutory contributions and is defined as one plus social security contributions' share of total wages and salaries. Data sources are national Quarterly National Accounts and Labour Statistics. Data is seasonally adjusted, semi-annual and the estimation period was 1971 II to 1985 I. Given the simultaneous determination of wages and prices, all equations were estimated by a two-stage least square method with independent variables and growth of bank lending used as instruments.

The results

A number of alternative hypothesis were tested. For the standard Phillips curve specification, where nominal wages are explained only by inflation and the unemployment rate, the most unsatisfactory feature was that the coefficient of inflation term came far below the expected unity. Inclusion of productivity as an additional explanatory variable increased the long-run elasticity of prices to wages to about 0.70. Hence the standard version as well as the equation with productivity variable were estimated with the price elasticity constrained to 1.

In addition to the productivity variable, the change in terms of trade, the change in profits and employer's social security contribution rate were also tried as explanatory variables. Since terms of trade and profit variables, however, compete with the productivity variable, the equations did not perform

Table AII.1. **The Phillips-curve**[1]

	c	u	$\ln(u) -$ $\ln(u^*)$	p[2]	q[3]	SEE	DW	$\bar{R}^2$
Free estimation:								
Basic Phillips-curve	7.29	−0.81		0.55		1.80	2.76	0.59
	(2.44)	(2.67)		(1.69)				
With productivity term	4.95	−0.71		0.71	0.71	1.80	2.66	0.59
	(1.03)	(1.91)		(1.58)	(1.00)			
Hysteresis[4]	2.80		−3.98	1.09	0.60	1.69	2.58	0.63
	(0.20)		(3.82)	(4.80)	(2.74)			
Constrained estimation:								
Basic Phillips-curve (Version A)	3.51	−0.52		1.0		1.95	2.29	0.15
	(3.27)	(2.41)		(−)				
With productivity term (Version B)	2.12	−0.49		1.0	0.91	1.84	2.40	0.24
	(1.73)	(2.39)		(−)	(2.04)			

1. The dependent variable is the growth of the private sector wage rate. All equations are estimated by two-stage least squares on seasonally-adjusted semi-annual data, per cent changes refer to semi-annual changes. The explanatory variables are constant (c), unemployment rate (u), inflation term (p) and productivity growth (q). The estimation period is 1971 II to 1985 I.
2. Specified as two-semester moving average (based on private consumption deflator) for basic Phillips-curve in free estimation and three-semester moving average for other specifications.
3. Specified as three-semester moving average for constraint estimation and four-semester moving average for free estimation, respectively.
4. The unemployment term is defined as a difference between the actual unemployment rate and eight-semester moving average unemployment rate lagged by one semester.
Source: OECD Secretariat.

better, even though the additional variables had have the expected sign and were also near significant. The employer's social security contribution rate was significant with a sign suggesting backward-shifting into nominal wages.

An alternative equation was estimated incorporating the so-called hysteresis hypothesis[2]. In this specification the natural rate is not constant but is a function of past values of the actual rate of unemployment. Nominal wages react to the difference between the actual unemployment rate and the natural rate, defined here as an eight semester moving average of the lagged unemployment rate. In this case there exists no NAIRU, as the present unemployment is a function of its own past history. The specification suggests segmented labour markets, which may be explained for instance by destructive effects of unemployment on human capital or insider-outsider roles of employees[3] in the wage bargaining process. (Table 1).

Real and nominal wage rigidities

Two specific measures of wage rigidity may be derived from estimated nominal wage equations. The *real wage rigidity* is defined as the short-run elasticity of nominal wages with respect to inflation divided by short-run semi-elasticity of nominal wages with respect to the unemployment rate. Thus the real wages are more flexible, the less rapidly nominal wages respond to a price shock and/or the more responsive they are to the unemployment rate. (Table 2).

Table AII.2. **Real and nominal wage rigidity**

	Unemploy-ment rate	Elasticity of nominal wages			Real wage rigidity	
		Prices		Unemploy-ment rate	Short run	Long run
		Short run	Long run			
		1	2	3	$4 = \frac{1}{3}$	$5 = \frac{2}{3}$
Finland (Version A)	any	0.33	1	0.52	0.63	1.92
Finland (Version B)[1]	any	0.33	1	0.49	0.42	0.71
Finland, hysteresis	3.82	0.52	1.03	2.10	0.25	–
	6.0	0.52	1.03	1.65	0.32	
United States	any	0.22	1.01	0.33	0.67	3.06
Japan	1.7	0.93	0.93	3.31	0.28	0.28
Australia[2]	any	0.45	0.90	1.78	0.25	..
Germany[3]	..	..	..	..	1.05	1.16
Austria	3.9	0.48	0.97	0.58	0.83	1.67

1. For calculation of rigidity measures with productivity term, see Coe. D.-Gagliardi F., "Nominal wage determination in ten OECD economies", OECD/ESD Working Paper No. 19, 1985.
2. Hysteresis specification.
3. With productivity term.

The price equation

The estimated price equation is a standard cost mark-up type (equation 2), where the explanatory variables are nominal wages, employers' social security contribution rate, productivity, import prices and food prices, the latter included as additional explanatory variable because of the administrative price setting system in Finland. Indeed, without the separate food price variable, the sum of the coefficients of cost variables failed to add up close to unity, which is an important requirement of cost mark-up price equation to be an accurate description of price formation process. Another signficant condition of the cost push argument is, that an inflation response to wages offset by respective increases in productivity requires equality between the coefficients of labour cost and the productivity variable. In free estimation, where nominal labour cost and productivity were introduced as separate variables, this condition was fulfilled, but the standard error of productivity parameter remained too high. Therefore, these two parameters were reduced to one variable, the unit labour costs, in the final specification (Table 3).

Table AII.3. **The price equation[1]**

	c	w	q	pm	pf	SEE	DW	$\bar{R}^2$
Free estimation	−0.16	0.46	−0.44	0.26	0.19	1.08	2.32	0.80
	(0.16)	(3.71)	(1.20)	(4.96)	(1.36)			
Constraint estimation[2]	−0.11	0.46		0.26	0.19	1.06	2.32	0.81
	(0.17)	(3.99)		(5.71)	(1.42)			

1. The dependent variable is the growth of the private consumption deflator, net of indirect taxes. The explanatory variables are constant (c), growth of private sector labour costs (w) including the employer's social security contributions, the growth of productivity (q), the changes of import prices (pm) and the changes of food prices (pf). The data is semi-annual and seasonally adjusted. The estimation period is 1972 II to 1985 I.
2. Constraining the coefficients of w and q to equal, implies that the explanatory variable is a unit labour cost variable.
Source: OECD Secretariat.

Stability tests

On *a priori* grounds, one could expect some behavioural changes in the wage and price equations especially after the first oil shock when the unemployment level rose significantly and the role of import prices increased as oil prices had nearly tripled. Recessive regressions were run on all equations to test for instability and the CUSUM and CUSUMQ statistics of the residuals were calculated. Based on CUSUM statistics stability is accepted in all equations but the CUSUMQ statistics indicates instability at the 5 per cent level in basic Phillips curve specification with and without productivity term, whereas stability is accepted in the hysteresis specification. The Quandt likelihood ratio statistic suggests the possibility of a break in behaviour in 1977 to 1978 and again in 1981 to 1982. In the price equation, the possible break in behaviour has probably happened already after the first oil shock, since the Quandt's likelihood ratio peaks at the first semester in 1976.

NOTES AND REFERENCES

1. This presentation follows that in Coe (1985) *op. cit.,* where pe $= \Sigma$ L3ip$_{t-i}$.

2. Coe (1985), *op. cit.*

3. Blanchard J and Summers L.H., *"Hysteresis and the European unemployment problem"*, paper presented in the NBER macro conference, April 1986.

CHRONOLOGY OF MAIN ECONOMIC POLICY MEASURES

1985

1st January

Bank of Finland aligns interest rate on short-term export credits with Bank's base rate and reduces maximum annual average credit from Mk 30 million to Mk 20 million

11th January

Call money market rate lowered from 14.8 per cent to 14.6 per cent.

25th January

Call money market rate reduced from 14.6 per cent to 14.2 per cent.

1st February

Bank of Finland base rate lowered from 9.5 per cent to 9 per cent. Most regulated interest rates decline accordingly.

26th February

Call money market rate reduced from 14.2 per cent to 14.0 per cent.

1st March

The Bank of Finland entitles authorised banks to conclude option contracts subject to certain conditions. However, contracts may not, until further notice, concern rates of exchange quoted against the Finnish markka.

21st March

The Government decided, in principle, on an economic-policy line of action designed to combat inflation. Endeavour will be made in the 1986 budget to limit the rise in expenditure to a maximum of 1 per cent. A tight spending policy is intended to provide scope for tax cuts and to make it possible to raise central government prices and charges very little. A favourable and well-balanced course of developments in the most important purpose categories will be ensured by a reallocation of expenditures. The Government proposes that a temporary rise of 0.5 pennies in electricity tax and that the employer's child allowance contribution of 0.5 percentage point be abolished from 1st November 1985. The intention is to cut long-distance call charges from the same date by 10 per cent.

10th April

To remove price linkages due to price controls and to improve functioning of price surveillance, number of goods subject to notification procedure is reduced. Concurrently, pricing principles related to this procedure are revised, so that efforts will be made to shift from branch-specific price calculations gradually to firm-specific analysis.

63

23rd April

Protocol on municipal finances (see 4th July 1984) is signed. Division of costs between state and municipalities is kept such as it is according to decisions now in force. Municipalities and inter-municipal authorities should prepare their budgets so that local tax rates need not be raised. The scope for manœuvre in state finances makes it possible to develop activities in such a way that general government aid payable to municipalities will increase by 2 per cent on average. Within the framework set by financial possibilities, consumption expenditure could also be increased in real terms by a maximum of 2 per cent. The increase in personnel should not exceed 2 per cent. Regarding wage and salary costs, the local government sector should be prepared for increases to the order of 1½ per cent in new agreements. As regards costs other than those due to wages and salaries, an average rise of 4 per cent can be used in budgets.

26th April

The call money rate lowered to 13.8 per cent.

14th May

The Government delivers economic policy statement to Parliament. No notable changes in the longer-term economic policy line of action are required by economic developments or prospects for the next few years. Growth seems to continue satisfactorily and steadily for longer than previously forecast, and it is not yet advisable to include expansionary measures in the 1986 budget. A notably easier fiscal policy stance can be adopted only after inflation has been brought down sufficiently. The target set is that inflation should not exceed 4 per cent in 1986.

10th June

Municipalities may during periods of upswing and boom deposit funds make so-called municipal countercyclical deposits to be used later for financing investments during periods of downswing and recession. Interest and supplementary interest will be paid on these deposits from state funds. The arrangement does not relate to inter-municipal authorities.

13th June

Investment fund transfers made from accounting periods that ended before 1979 may be used during the period 1st October 1985 to 31st December 1987.

24th June

The Bank of Finland prohibits, until further notice, the sale abroad of certain kinds of debt instruments listed on the Helsinkin Stock Exchange.

26th June

The call money rate lowered to 13.6 per cent.

12th July

In the first supplementary budget, expenditure totals Mk 1 139 million and revenue Mk 650 million. More than half of total expenditure is due to the replacement of two foreign loans by more advantageous ones, and means no actual addition to expenditure. In order to decelerate inflation, the motor-car and motor-cycle tax was cut, as from 6th May 1985. Borrowing authority was raised by Mk 580 million.

26th July

An individual early pension may be granted to a person aged 55 or over if his working capacity has deteriorated so that he cannot reasonably be expected to earn a living. An earlier-than-normal old age pension may be granted to a person aged 60, the rate of pension being then correspondingly lower. Both schemes enter into force on 1st January 1986.

15th August

The call money rate lowered to 13.3 per cent.

1st September

The guidelines for authorised foreign exchange dealers concerning operations on forward exchange markets are changed. Guidelines specify in greater detail than before conditions for participating in forward exchange markets and tie forward exchange contracts more closely to foreign exchange rate risks.

17th September

The call money rate lowered to 12.9 per cent.

18th September

The 1986 budget proposal submitted to Parliament. Expenditure totals Mk 100.8 billion (7.4 per cent higher than the 1985 ordinary budget) and revenue, Mk 89.5 billion (up 6.7 per cent). The borrowing requirement is Mk 11.3 billion.

1st October

Local governments obliged to place counter-cyclical revenue deposits in State Office between 1st October 1985 to 2nd May 1986. The deposits bear a 5½ per cent interest rate and are allowed to be withdrawn between 1st October 1986 to 31st August 1987.

18th October

The call money market rate lowered to 12.6 per cent.

5th November

The call money market rate lowered to 12.4 per cent.

26th November

The call money market rate lowered to 12.0 per cent.

5th December

Second supplementary budget incorporates net additional expenditure of Mk 1 678 million.

13th December

Banks' cash reserve requirement reduced from 5.6 per cent to 5.3 per cent.

27th December

The call money market rate lowered to 11.7 per cent.

1986

1st January

Finland became a full member of the European Free Trade Association (EFTA).

Electricity tax changed to 1.6 penni per Kwh.

Private sector employer's national pension contribution fixed at 4.45 per cent, 5.40 per cent or 5.95 per cent and the sickness insurance contribution at 1.45 per cent of the wage and salary bill for 1986 (public sector rates are 4.95 per cent, 5.95 per cent and 2.45 per cent to 3.45 per cent respectively). Health insurance and national pension contribution rates set at 1.70 per cent and 1.80 per cent respectively of income liable to local government taxation. The local government participation to the costs of national pensions fixed at 0.93 per cent per unit of local taxation. Average employer's pension contribution is set at 12.2 per cent of wage bill.

Employer unemployment insurance contribution rate set at 0.95 per cent for 1986.

The Bank of Finland's base rate lowered from 9 per cent to 8½ per cent. Call money market system revised by fixing lower rate of interest on deposits then charged on call money advances.

The renewal of the Foreign Exchange Act. The penalty surcharge scheme applied to short-term import credits abolished. Investments in securities quoted abroad and in the form of funds held in accounts with foreign monetary institutions permitted up to a maximum of Mk 10 000 a year per resident. The upper limit on foreign exchange which may be acquired for the purchase of a second home abroad raised to Mk 600 000. Authorised banks were granted the right to sell travel exchange without upper limit on the basis of a breakdown of costs drawn up by the purchaser of travel exchange. Securities brokers accorded the same rights as the authorised banks to act as intermediaries in securities transactions between residents and non-residents.

Business taxation reform reduced enterprises income tax rate from 43 per cent to 33 per cent. The undervaluation rate of stocks reduced from 50 per cent to 40 per cent and the maximum amount of operating reserve allowances was raised to 25 per cent for 1986 and 30 per cent for 1987.

2nd January

The rate on call money deposits lowered to 11 per cent.

17th January

1986 budget approved. Outlays estimated at Mk 101.4 billion (up to 8.1 per cent on the ordinary budget) and revenue at Mk 89.5 billion (up 6.7 per cent), leaving a borrowing requirement of Mk 12.0 billion. Inflation adjustment of personal income tax brackets by 8 per cent and a substantial alleviation of wealth taxation. Fuel taxes raised by 4 per cent to 5 per cent but natural gas taxation unchanged. Child allowances raised by 4 per cent effective from 1st October 1986. Railway tariffs and postal rates raised by 4 per cent to 5 per cent. Retail prices of alcohol raised by 4 per cent from 1st January 1986.

25th February

Cash reserve requirement reduced from 5.0 per cent to 4.7 per cent.

1st March

Bank of Finland's base rate lowered to 8 per cent.

3rd March

Call money rate lowered to 11.2 per cent and the rate on call money deposits lowered to 10.5 per cent respectively.

White collar employees sign a two-year incomes policy contract, in effect to the end of February 1988. The pay increase is 2 per cent in the first year of the contract and 2¼ per cent from 1st March 1987. An index clause (without any adjustment for changes in the terms of trade) incorporated in the settlement. Working hours to be shortened as from 1987 by eight hours in year and another eight hours as from 1988.

15th March

Blue collar workers accept an incomes policy agreement. The agreement provides a pay increase of 55 penni per hour or at least 1.5 per cent in the first year and as from 1st March 1987 64 penni per hour. Branchwise adjustment reserve set at 0.3 per cent of the wage bill. An index clause adopted from the white collar settlement incorporated. Working hours to be shortened as from 1987 to 1989 by sixteen hours in each year and by twenty hours in 1990.

The economic policy package, introduced in connection with incomes policy agreements, comprises increased public construction, 20 000 dwellings with financial support in 1987, increased unemployment benefits and child allowances, improved day care services, better adult education and full inflation adjustment in personal income tax brackets in 1987.

A supplementary economic policy package introduced to revive investment and employment. Investment reserves from 1984 released, energy taxation renewed and export promotion grants increased. Energy taxation to be changed on value-added basis.

26th March

Income agreement for agriculture include increase in target prices and price policy support of Mk 132 million in 1986 and Mk 269 million as from 1st March 1987.

13th May

The call money rate raised to 13 per cent and the rate on call money advances to 12.3 per cent.

14th May

The call money rate raised to 16 per cent and the rate on call money advances to 15.3 per cent.

15th May

The Bank of Finland raised the currency index by 2.5 points to 105.

16th May

The call money rate lowered to 14 per cent and rate on call money advances to 13.3 per cent.

19th May

The Bank of Finland's base rate lowered from 8 per cent to 7 per cent.

20th May

The call money rate lowered first to 13 per cent and later, during the same day, to 12 per cent. Respective rates on call money advances were 12.3 per cent and 11.3 per cent.

21st May

The agreement on stumpage prices to come into effect between 1st April 1986 and 31st March 1989. In the first year, stumpage prices lowered 4.5 per cent. Prices hereafter tied to the export price of the forestry industry.

22nd May

The call money rate lowered to 11 per cent and the rate on call money advances to 10.3 per cent.

STATISTICAL ANNEX

Selected background statistics

	Average 1976-85	1976	1977	1978	1979	1980	1981	1982	1983	1984	1985
A. Percent change from previous year											
At constant 1980 prices											
Private consumption	2.4	0.9	-1.2	2.8	5.6	1.9	1.4	4.1	2.7	3.0	3.2
Gross fixed capital formation	0.5	-8.8	-5.1	-7.2	3.1	9.9	3.2	3.5	4.8	-1.5	3.2
Public investment	2.2	-4.2	0.6	0.7	2.0	6.2	2.5	8.6	3.9	-1.2	3.3
Private investment	1.0	-8.0	4.9	-8.3	3.3	10.4	3.3	2.8	4.9	-1.6	3.1
GDP	3.0	0.3	0.2	2.6	7.4	5.6	1.8	3.0	2.9	3.0	2.8
GDP price deflator	9.3	12.6	10.2	7.7	8.2	9.2	11.4	9.2	9.0	9.0	6.5
Industrial production	3.8	1.0	0.5	5.1	10.7	7.8	2.4	0.8	3.0	4.9	2.6
Employment	0.5	-2.3	-2.0	-1.5	2.6	3.1	1.1	1.0	0.6	1.0	1.1
Compensation of employees (current prices)	12.0	15.6	8.0	5.2	14.4	17.1	15.7	10.8	10.8	11.3	10.9
Productivity (GDP/employment)	2.5	2.6	2.2	4.1	4.7	2.4	0.7	2.0	2.3	2.0	1.7
Unit labour costs (compensation/GDP)	9.0	15.3	7.8	2.5	7.0	11.5	13.9	7.8	7.9	8.2	8.1
B. Percentage ratios											
Gross fixed capital formation as % of GDP at constant prices	26.0	29.5	27.9	25.2	24.3	25.3	25.6	25.7	26.2	25.0	25.1
Stockbuiding as % of GDP at constant prices	0.3	-1.4	-1.6	-2.1	2.4	3.3	0.5	0.7	0.5	0.7	-0.1
Foreign balance as % of GDP at constant prices	0.0	-6.6	-2.0	1.7	-0.9	-0.8	2.4	1.2	1.2	2.8	1.2
Compensation of employees as % of GDP at current prices	55.0	58.2	57.0	54.3	53.4	54.3	55.6	54.9	54.3	53.8	54.5
Direct taxes as percent of household income	16.8	18.8	17.9	15.9	15.2	15.8	16.9	16.4	16.5	17.1	17.3
Household saving as percent of disposable income	4.8	4.5	3.8	4.9	4.6	5.3	4.3	5.1	5.6	5.0	4.5
Unemployment as percent of civilian labour force	5.8	3.9	5.9	7.3	6.0	4.7	5.2	5.9	6.1	6.2	6.3
C. Other indicator											
Current balance (billion US$)	-1.1	-1.1	-0.1	0.6	-0.2	-1.4	-0.4	-0.8	-0.9	0.0	-0.6

Sources: Central Statistical Office, *National accounts*; Ministry of Labour, *Labour Reports*; and OECD, *Main Economic Indicators.*

Table A. **Supply and use of resources**
Mk. million, current prices

	1977	1978	1979	1980	1981	1982	1983	1984[1]	1985[1]
Consumers' expenditure on goods and services	72 477	80 231	91 494	104 038	118 016	134 161	149 607	164 677	179 980
General government current expenditure on goods and services	24 006	26 346	29 876	34 895	40 837	46 661	53 305	59 664	67 467
Gross fixed capital formation	35 106	34 413	38 689	48 638	54 686	60 987	68 987	72 408	79 130
Change in stocks	−1 832	−2 797	3 610	6 287	1 144	2 001	1 690	2 010	−351
Total domestic demand	129 757	138 193	163 669	193 858	214 683	243 810	273 569	298 759	326 226
Exports of goods and services (non-factor)	36 974	42 960	52 486	63 386	73 321	76 397	84 061	95 645	98 700
Imports of goods and services (non-factor)	34 727	37 390	49 948	65 016	70 239	74 367	82 770	87 833	95 000
Statistical discrepancy	−2 003	−143	752	328	690	−668	−424	1 743	7 655
Gross domestic product in purchasers' values	130 001	143 620	166 959	192 556	218 455	245 172	274 436	308 314	337 581

1. Provisional.
Source : Central Statistical Office, *National Accounts.*

Table B. Supply and use of ressources
Mk. million, 1980 prices

	1977	1978	1979	1980	1981	1982	1983	1984[1]	1985[1]
Consumers' expenditure on goods and services	94 039	96 648	102 096	104 038	105 494	109 825	112 793	116 208	119 931
General government current expenditure on goods and services	30 989	32 248	33 435	34 895	36 289	37 585	39 080	40 200	41 919
Gross fixed capital formation	46 247	42 919	44 270	48 638	50 195	51 962	54 428	53 596	55 282
Change in stocks	-2 591	-3 684	4 376	6 287	1 019	1 504	1 087	1 432	-113
Total domestic demand	168 684	168 131	184 177	193 858	192 997	200 876	207 388	211 436	217 019
Exports of goods and services (non-factor)	49 397	53 595	58 428	63 386	67 462	66 438	68 898	72 932	73 190
Imports of goods and services (non-factor)	52 730	50 676	60 044	65 016	62 720	64 026	66 346	67 136	70 590
Statistical discrepancy	145	-1 311	-258	328	-1 711	-1 457	-2 188	-3 188	439
Gross domestic product in purchasers' values	165 496	169 739	182 303	192 556	196 028	201 831	207 752	214 044	220 058

1. Provisional.
Source: Central Statistical Office, National Accounts.

Tableau C. Gross domestic product by industry of origin
Mk. million, 1980 prices

	1977	1978	1979	1980	1981	1982	1983	1984[1]
Agriculture, hunting, forestry and fishing	13 656	13 694	15 397	16 573	15 404	15 522	16 139	16 534
Mining and quarrying	745	773	829	861	886	992	990	972
Manufacturing	38 433	40 289	44 791	48 408	49 740	50 150	51 864	54 406
Electricity, gas and water	4 206	4 473	4 779	4 991	5 211	5 141	5 367	5 737
Construction	13 019	12 787	12 867	13 654	13 491	14 189	14 712	14 260
Transport, storage and communications	11 288	11 616	12 891	13 644	14 094	14 234	14 703	15 005
Wholesale and retail trade, restaurants and hotels	17 885	18 224	19 551	20 268	20 456	21 257	21 496	21 986
Finance, insurance, real estate, and business services	20 399	21 356	22 373	23 953	25 350	26 564	28 102	29 932
of which: Owner occupied dwellings	9 909	10 350	10 713	11 072	11 414	11 724	12 050	12 335
Producers of government services	22 402	23 373	24 359	25 273	26 444	27 460	28 302	29 002
Other community, social, and personal services	9 031	9 062	9 335	9 565	9 828	10 104	10 435	10 716
less: Imputed bank service change	3 899	4 079	4 279	4 678	5 021	5 257	5 615	6 356
Net commodity taxes, and other correction items	18 331	18 171	19 424	20 044	20 237	21 347	21 257	21 850
Gross domestic product in purchasers' values	165 496	169 739	182 303	192 556	196 028	201 831	207 752	214 044

1. Provisional.
Source: Central Statistical Office, National Accounts.

Table D. Central government revenue and expenditure (new SNA)
Mk. million

	1981	1982	1983	1984[1]	1985[1]
Current revenue	48 999	54 928	61 745	72 182	80 904
Direct taxes	15 816	16 953	19 298	22 225	25 530
Indirect taxes	29 694	33 206	36 975	43 527	47 797
Income from property and entrepreneurship	935	1 944	2 345	2 641	3 031
Other domestic current transfers	2 554	2 825	3 127	3 789	4 546
Current expenditure	44 949	51 218	61 121	67 444	75 480
Purchase of goods and services	12 937	15 047	17 371	18 376	20 584
Subsidies	6 896	7 349	8 437	9 305	9 799
Property income payable	1 577	2 171	3 096	3 824	4 669
Current transfers	23 539	26 651	32 217	35 939	40 428
To other public authorities	13 293	15 632	19 363	21 773	25 974
To households	9 163	10 417	12 185	13 300	13 504
To the rest of the world	453	512	669	866	950
Net current saving	4 671	3 789	611	4 722	5 407
Depreciation	848	938	1 056	1 095	1 227
Gross saving	5 514	4 727	1 667	5 817	6 634
Gross fixed capital formation	2 878	3 268	3 822	3 737	4 012
Purchases of land, net	203	170	216	216	315
Increase in stocks	−335	119	380	244	167
Surplus on current and fixed investment account	2 768	1 170	2 751	1 620	2 140
Capital transfers to other sectors, net	−1 062	−1 562	−1 276	−1 434	−1 591
Net lending	1 706	−392	−4 027	186	549

1. Provisional.
Source: Central Statistical Office, *National Accounts.*

Table E. **Balance of payments**
US $ million

	1977	1978	1979	1980	1981	1982	1983	1984[1]	1985[1]
Exports, fob	7 637	8 508	11 098	14 114	13 978	13 046	12 187	13 098	13 430
Imports, fob	7 193	7 417	10 715	14 760	13 556	12 808	12 036	11 607	12 515
Trade balance	443	1 091	384	-646	421	238	151	1 491	915
Services, net	-500	-374	-429	-634	-709	-913	-948	-1 334	-1 511
Balance on goods and services	-57	717	-45	-1 279	-287	-675	-797	157	-596
Private transfers, net	-12	-15	-16	-20	-10	-27	-23	-22	-8
Official transfers, net	-38	-37	-95	-102	-116	-107	-120	-152	-153
Current balance	-106	665	-156	-1 401	-403	-810	-940	-17	-757
Long-term capital	454	901	242	49	557	633	352	674	1 302
Private	346	784	-40	-61	394	404	244	577	1 087
Official[2]	108	117	282	110	162	229	109	97	215
Basic balance	347	1 566	86	-1 353	154	-177	-588	674	545
Short-term capital	..	..	..	..	..	..	..	..	..
Non-monetary	..	..	..	..	..	..	..	..	..
Private monetary institutions	..	..	..	..	..	..	..	..	..
Errors and omissions	..	..	..	..	..	..	..	..	..
Net transactions of monetary authorities	-272	1 035	127	256	407	-24	-253	1 581	622
Use of IMF credit	–	-43	-111	–	-17	-41	-15	–	–
Miscellaneous official accounts[3]	..	..	..	..	..	..	..	..	..
Allocations of SDRs	..	..	..	..	..	..	..	..	..
Change in reserves[4] (+ = augmentation)	51	670	340	318	-210	223	-217	1 716	612

1. Provisional.
2. Includes government bond issues.
3. Includes payments agreements (tied currencies).
4. Convertible reserves.
Source: Finish submission to OECD.

74

Table F. Labour market

	Labour Force Surveys			Employment Exchange Service		
				Unemployed persons seeking work		Unfilled vacancies
	Labour force	Employment	Unemployment (per cent of total labour force)	Total	Insured	
	1 000 persons		Per cent	1 000 persons		'000
1977	2 371	2 232	5.9	132.5	59.3	6.4
1978	2 372	2 200	7.3	175.2	71.5	5.5
1979	2 399	2 256	6.0	150.3	54.9	8.3
1980	2 442	2 328	4.7	109.5	37.4	12.2
1981	2 481	2 353	5.1	115.4	49.6	13.0
1982	2 526	2 377	5.9	138.1	61.6	11.3
1983	2 546	2 390	6.1	143.9	64.7	11.8
1984	2 572	2 413	6.2	135.3	60.1	12.0
1985	2 600	2 437	6.3	141.5	64.0	12.2
			Seasonally-adjusted			
Quarterly:						
1983 1	2 541	2 386	6.1	142.5	76.8	10.8
2	2 550	2 387	6.3	142.3	58.7	11.2
3	2 535	2 384	5.9	145.4	57.9	12.1
4	2 559	2 400	6.2	143.0	65.6	12.7
1984 1	2 510	2 340	6.0	138.1	71.2	12.4
2	2 616	2 455	6.3	135.6	56.0	11.9
3	2 636	2 488	6.1	134.2	53.0	11.7
4	2 527	2 371	6.3	133.9	60.3	12.0
1985 1	2 531	2 359	6.1	135.0	71.2	12.2
2	2 646	2 483	6.2	141.2	58.4	12.0
3	2 658	2 502	6.3	142.8	58.0	12.3
4	..	..	6.5	..	..	12.5

Sources: Ministry of Labour, *Labour Reports.*

Table G. Imports: Prices, volume and value by commodity group

	Import unit values 1980 = 100					Volume of imports 1980 = 100					Value of imports (cif) Mk. million				
	Total	Raw materials, etc.	Fuels and lubricants	Investment goods	Consumer goods	Total	Raw materials, etc.	Fuels and lubricants	Investment goods	Consumer goods	Total	Raw materials, etc.	Fuels and lubricants	Investment goods	Consumer goods
1978	74	71	52	89	92	75	75	104	67	92	32 338	20 431	2 224	4 801	4 830
1979	86	83	81	94	96	89	90	103	76	86	44 222	28 878	3 401	5 720	6 133
1980	100	100	100	100	100	100	100	100	100	100	58 250	38 622	4 088	7 989	7 440
1981	112	113	127	105	108	94	90	99	106	100	61 269	39 156	5 115	8 877	8 015
1982	117	117	132	111	114	95	91	90	104	108	64 751	41 144	4 869	9 195	9 130
1983	125	124	129	124	126	98	93	95	110	113	71 528	44 757	5 006	10 860	10 572
1984	131	131	132	128	132	98	93	93	107	116	74 682	47 028	5 034	10 993	11 454
1985	135	134	129	134	142	104	99	104	109	123	81 407	50 845	5 492	11 671	12 966
Quarterly:															
1983 1	125	124	135	120	126	90	85	60	105	118	16 356	10 151	1 824	2 507	2 772
2	124	123	125	124	130	95	90	81	114	114	17 292	10 622	1 034	2 830	2 733
3	127	126	128	125	130	97	91	130	103	99	17 849	11 096	1 701	2 558	2 384
4	128	127	131	127	128	108	105	108	116	113	20 031	12 888	1 448	2 965	2 684
1984 1	129	129	130	127	131	90	81	76	111	120	16 957	10 107	1 019	2 811	2 936
2	130	129	129	127	134	99	97	95	108	108	18 734	12 041	1 250	2 740	2 689
3	133	133	132	131	136	99	97	112	94	109	19 227	12 441	1 518	2 466	2 766
4	134	134	136	130	138	101	96	90	114	120	19 730	12 437	1 248	2 977	3 063
1985 1	138	138	145	133	142	93	88	50	104	125	18 818	11 735	739	2 745	3 252
2	137	136	141	131	145	106	104	100	114	117	21 291	13 687	1 431	2 990	3 161
3	134	133	122	135	143	100	94	127	99	121	19 542	12 044	1 587	2 665	3 202
4	132	128	123	139	146	113	108	138	118	124	21 755	13 378	1 735	3 270	3 351

Sources: Board of Customs, *Foreign Trade.*

76

Table H. **Exports: Prices, volume and value by commodity group**

| | Prices 1980 = 100 | | | | Volume of exports 1980 = 100 | | | | Value of exports (fob) Mk. million | | | Manufactured products | | | |
| | | | | | | | | | | Agriculture and forestry | Total | of which: | | | |
	Total	Wood	Paper	Metal and engin.	Total	Wood	Paper	Metal and engin.	Total			Total	Wood	Paper	Metal and engin.
1978	80	76	79	89	84	79	84	93	35 206	838		34 219	4 641	10 402	9 593
1979	90	84	88	92	92	93	94	97	43 430	1 203		41 922	6 073	12 992	10 342
1980	100	100	100	100	100	100	100	100	52 795	1 221		51 260	7 742	15 751	11 547
1981	111	105	112	116	103	85	97	111	60 308	1 787		58 231	6 852	17 127	14 858
1982	119	105	119	133	100	77	93	124	63 026	1 400		61 199	6 278	17 502	18 908
1983	127	116	121	145	104	77	101	121	69 692	1 430		67 919	6 944	19 327	20 211
1984	134	124	134	145	114	74	112	138	80 904	2 550		77 996	7 145	23 573	22 998
1985	138	118	137	149	115	74	116	141	84 022	2 381		81 209	6 728	25 046	24 401
Quarterly:															
1983 1	126	114	120	148	101	73	93	120	16 812	649		16 078	1 609	4 400	5 107
2	126	116	120	146	103	81	95	121	17 181	322		16 767	1 824	4 514	5 093
3	127	114	123	144	97	72	103	107	16 259	98		16 086	1 588	4 985	4 448
4	128	116	123	146	115	85	112	132	19 441	361		18 988	1 922	5 429	5 562
1984 1	132	119	127	146	114	72	106	141	19 772	847		18 855	1 668	5 318	5 957
2	133	124	131	146	113	77	112	124	19 775	665		19 018	1 840	5 775	5 243
3	137	127	138	146	108	72	112	125	19 451	568		18 790	1 775	6 087	5 256
4	137	126	140	144	121	77	116	157	21 905	470		21 333	1 864	6 394	6 541
1985 1	140	125	140	150	108	65	113	122	20 107	919		19 114	1 569	6 200	5 277
2	139	118	139	150	121	83	118	150	22 502	715		21 635	1 890	6 427	6 763
3	138	116	137	152	114	67	122	140	20 667	349		20 207	1 514	2 559	6 119
4	134	115	131	153	117	79	113	142	20 746	397		20 252	1 755	5 860	6 243

Sources : Central Statistical Office, *Bulletin of Statistics.*

Table I. Foreign trade by area
Million US dollars, monthly averages

	1977	1978	1979	1980	1981	1982	1983	1984	1985
Imports, cif									
United States	29.7	32.9	47.7	75.7	88.9	68.4	60.8	51.7	59.0
United Kingdom	55.1	59.9	81.7	111.8	95.3	81.5	71.3	79.9	78.5
Sweden	85.0	94.2	130.8	157.1	133.6	136.1	119.7	127.5	129.1
Norway	23.4	18.1	24.0	27.4	29.5	23.9	28.2	21.6	26.3
Germany (Fed. Rep.)	87.0	88.2	122.1	164.2	143.8	148.5	141.6	144.0	163.4
Other OECD	131.6	141.1	201.9	271.6	247.7	252.9	262.3	259.7	284.8
Total OECD	411.8	434.4	608.2	807.8	738.8	711.3	683.8	684.4	741.1
Centrally-planned economies	151.9	152.2	221.2	324.3	320.4	315.4	309.1	271.4	262.7
Other	71.5	67.6	112.9	169.0	123.9	92.3	77.1	79.8	89.3
World	635.2	654.2	942.3	1 301.1	1 183.1	1 119.0	1 070.0	1 035.6	1 093.1
Exports, fob									
United States	28.3	28.1	39.6	37.3	43.2	34.7	42.8	91.8	71.2
United Kingdom	75.8	89.7	121.5	132.7	124.0	118.1	107.7	135.0	121.9
Sweden	100.6	104.1	149.2	194.8	155.6	130.5	129.2	138.1	148.8
Norway	34.7	35.8	50.0	49.3	54.8	52.9	35.6	50.8	47.2
Germany (Fed. Rep.)	64.5	71.8	102.2	125.3	106.4	98.5	99.8	107.5	104.5
Other OECD	136.6	161.9	227.2	274.3	248.5	230.0	233.1	254.9	264.0
Total OECD	440.5	491.4	689.7	813.7	732.5	664.7	648.2	778.1	757.6
Centrally-planned economies	144.9	149.6	154.8	241.9	312.6	317.4	293.3	232.7	264.3
Other	54.6	71.6	84.6	123.6	119.6	107.1	102.1	111.3	106.3
World	640.0	712.6	929.1	1 179.2	1 164.7	1 089.2	1 043.6	1 122.1	1 128.2

Source: OECD, Foreign Trade Statistics, Series A.

Table J. Prices and wages, 1980 = 100

	Consumer prices				Wholesale prices			Building cost	Wage and salary earnings[1]				Government	
	Total	Food	Rent	Energy	Total	Domestic goods	Imported goods		Total	Industry	Workers	Private	Local	Central
1977	77	81	82	71	75	77	68	76	75	75	75	74	79	77
1978	83	85	87	75	79	80	76	80	80	81	80	80	83	81
1979	90	89	92	81	86	86	85	88	89	89	89	89	92	90
1980	100	100	100	100	100	100	100	100	100	100	100	100	100	100
1981	112	113	115	119	113	113	112	110	113	114	113	113	112	113
1982	123	127	128	129	121	123	116	118	125	126	125	125	126	124
1983	133	136	136	133	128	130	123	129	138	138	137	137	140	137
1984	142	146	143	133	135	138	130	137	151	151	150	151	155	147
1985	151	157	150	136	142	145	135	144	163	162	162	163	166	159
Quarterly:														
1983 1	128	131	131	134	126	127	121	124	132	133	131	131	133	132
2	132	137	136	133	126	128	121	128	138	139	137	138	139	137
3	135	137	138	133	129	130	125	131	138	138	137	138	141	137
4	137	138	138	133	130	132	126	133	144	143	142	143	147	143
1984 1	139	140	139	132	132	134	128	134	146	145	144	145	151	144
2	142	145	143	133	134	137	129	136	151	152	151	151	155	147
3	144	149	145	133	136	138	131	138	152	152	151	152	156	147
4	145	151	145	133	139	141	133	139	154	153	153	154	157	149
1985 1	148	153	146	135	142	144	137	141	158	157	157	157	162	155
2	151	159	150	136	143	146	137	144	165	164	164	164	167	160
3	152	159	152	136	142	146	135	145	165	163	163	165	167	160
4	152	158	153	137	141	145	133	146	166	164	165	167	168	161

1. 1983 and 1984 are preliminary estimates.
Sources: Central Statistical Office, Bulletin of Statistics; OECD, Main Economic Indicators.

Table K. Interest rates, money and credit

	Interest rates			Banks of Finland net claims on:					Money	
	Bank of Finland base rate	Call money rate	Average lending rate of commercial banks	Foreign sector	Public sector	Financial institutions	Corporate sector	Banks credit to the public	Money supply M1	M1 plus quasi money
	Per cent[1]			Mk. million, end of period						
1978	7.58	11.99	8.22	4 052	−571	1 175	1 592	61 997	11 496	60 682
1979	7.46	9.74	8.03	4 999	−1 203	1 495	2 117	72 047	14 087	71 157
1980	9.20	12.38	9.77	6 151	−1 266	1 611	2 421	83 270	14 979	81 601
1981	9.25	11.61	9.84	8 376	−942	−107	3 116	96 720	17 186	94 577
1982	8.81	11.99	9.33	9 083	−710	618	3 303	112 910	19 917	107 549
1983	9.00	15.14	9.56	7 951	−822	3 076	3 247	127 700	21 427	121 906
1984	9.50	16.53	10.49	17 576	−2 326	−2 713	2 032	144 710	24 945	141 658
1985	9.04	13.37	10.41	21 225	−3 277	−2 897	412	168 600	27 694	166 652
Quarterly:										
1984 1	9.50	17.50	10.35	12 304	960	−3 349	2 833	130 600	20 606	125 049
2	9.50	16.70	10.46	17 436	1 077	−6 671	1 930	134 500	22 026	129 549
3	9.50	16.37	10.52	15 254	501	−3 653	1 711	139 500	22 238	132 660
4	9.50	15.43	10.63	17 576	−2 326	−2 713	2 032	144 710	24 945	141 658
1985 1	9.17	14.26	10.45	19 494	−521	−7 741	1 666	150 150	22 152	145 638
2	9.00	13.84	10.37	21 642	−958	−8 414	855	154 900	24 750	153 455
3	9.00	13.38	10.42	19 720	−261	−5 376	566	161 000	26 092	156 195
4	9.00	12.37	10.40	21 225	−3 277	−2 897	412	168 600	27 694	166 652

1. Average for period.
2. Credits (in domestic currency) granted to the public by banks.
Sources: Bank of Finland, Monthly Bulletin; Central Statistical Office, Credit Market Statistics; and OECD, Main Economic Indicators.

BASIC STATISTICS :

INTERNATIONAL COMPARISONS

	Units	Reference period[1]	Australia	Austria
Population				
Total	Thousands	1985	15 752	7 555
Inhabitants per sq.km	Number		2	90
Net average annual increase over previous 10 years	%		1.3	0.0
Employment				
Total civilian employment (TCE)[2]	Thousands	1985	6 676	3 235 (8
of which: Agriculture	% of TCE		6.1	9.4
Industry	% of TCE		27.7	38.1
Services	% of TCE		66.2	52.5
Gross domestic product (GDP)				
At current prices and current exchange rates	Billion US$	1984	173.7	64.5
Per capita	US$		11 178	8 535
At current prices using current PPP's[3]	Billion US$	1984	..	85.7
Per capita	US$		..	11 345
Average annual volume growth over previous 5 years ...	%	1984	2.6	1.6
Gross fixed capital formation (GFCF)	% of GDP	1984	21.8	21.8
of which: Machinery and equipment	% of GDP		9.3 (83)	9.0
Residential construction	% of GDP		3.7 (83)	4.8
Average annual volume growth over previous 5 years ...	%	1984	1.3	–0.9
Gross saving ratio[4]	% of GDP	1984	20.3	24.1
General government				
Current expenditure on goods and services	% of GDP	1984	17.1	18.5
Current disbursements[5]	% of GDP	1984	32.6 (83)	44.8
Current receipts	% of GDP	1984	32.8 (83)	46.8
Net official development assistance	% of GNP	1984	0.46	0.28
Indicators of living standards				
Private consumption per capita using current PPP's[3] ...	US$	1984	6 742 *	6 490
Passenger cars, per 1 000 inhabitants	Number	1984	..	306 (8
Telephones, per 1 000 inhabitants	Number	1984	540 (83)	460 (8
Television sets, per 1 000 inhabitants	Number	1984	..	300 (8
Doctors, per 1 000 inhabitants	Number	1984	..	1.7 (8
Infant mortality per 1 000 live births	Number	1984	9.6 (83)	11.9 (8
Wages and prices (average annual increase over previous 5 years)				
Wages (earnings or rates according to availability)	%	1984	10.3	5.7
Consumer prices	%	1985	8.3	4.9
Foreign trade				
Exports of goods, fob*	Million US$	1985		17 220
as % of GDP	%			26.7
average annual increase over previous 5 years	%			–0.2
Imports of goods, cif*	Million US$	1985		20 964
as % of GDP	%			32.5
average annual increase over previous 5 years	%			–2.9
Total official reserves[6]	Million SDR's	1985	5 528	5 080
As ratio of average monthly imports of goods	Ratio		2.9	3.0

* At current prices and exchange rates.
1. Unless otherwise stated.
2. According to the definitions used in OECD *Labour force Statistics.*
3. PPP's = Purchasing Power Parities.
4. Gross saving = Gross national disposable income *minus* Private and Government consumption.
5. Current disbursements = Current expenditure on goods and services *plus* current transfers and payments of property income.
6. Gold included in reserves is valued at 35 SDR's per ounce. End of year.
7. Including Luxembourg.
8. Included in Belgium.
9. Including non-residential construction.

EMPLOYMENT OPPORTUNITIES

Economics and Statistics Department

OECD

A.   **Administrator.**   A number of economist positions may become available in 1986 in areas such as monetary and fiscal policy, balance of payments, resource allocation, macroeconomic policy issues, short-term forecasting and country studies. *Essential* qualifications and experience: advanced university degree in economics; good knowledge of statistical methods and applied econometrics; two or three years' experience in applied economic analysis; command of one of the two official languages (English and French). *Desirable* qualifications and experience also include: familiarity with the economic problems and data sources of a number of Member countries; proven drafting ability; experience with the estimation, simulation and implementation of computer-based economic models; some knowledge of the other official language.

B.   **Principal Administrator.**   A number of senior economist positions may become available in 1986 in areas such as monetary and fiscal policy, balance of payments, resource allocation, macroeconomic policy issues, short-term forecasting and country studies. *Essential* qualifications and experience: advanced university degree in economics; extensive experience in applied economic analysis, preferably with a central bank, economics/finance ministry or institute of economic research; good knowledge of statistical methods and applied econometrics; command of one of the two official languages (English and French) and proven drafting ability. *Desirable* qualifications and experience also include: experience in using economic analysis for formulating policy advice; familiarity with a number of OECD economies; experience in using econometric models; good knowledge of the other official language.

These positions carry a basic salary (tax free) from FF 193 968 or FF 239 328 (Administrator) and from FF 275 412 (Principal Administrator), supplemented by further additional allowances depending on residence and family situation.

Initial appointment will be on a two- or three-year fixed-term contract.

Vacancies are open to both male and female candidates from OECD Member countries. Applications citing reference "ECSUR", together with a detailed curriculum vitæ in English or French, should be sent to:

> Head of Personnel
> OECD
> 2, rue André-Pascal
> 75775 PARIS CEDEX 16
> France

OECD SALES AGENTS
DÉPOSITAIRES DES PUBLICATIONS DE L'OCDE

ARGENTINA - ARGENTINE
Carlos Hirsch S.R.L.,
Florida 165, 4º Piso,
(Galeria Guemes) 1333 Buenos Aires
Tel. 33.1787.2391 y 30.7122

AUSTRALIA-AUSTRALIE
D.A. Book (Aust.) Pty. Ltd.
11-13 Station Street (P.O. Box 163)
Mitcham, Vic. 3132   Tel. (03) 873 4411

AUSTRIA - AUTRICHE
OECD Publications and Information Centre,
4 Simrockstrasse,
5300 Bonn (Germany)   Tel. (0228) 21.60.45
Local Agent:
Gerold & Co., Graben 31, Wien 1 Tel. 52.22.35

BELGIUM - BELGIQUE
Jean de Lannoy, Service Publications OCDE,
avenue du Roi 202
B-1060 Bruxelles   Tel. 02/538.51.69

CANADA
Renouf Publishing Company Limited/
Éditions Renouf Limitée Head Office/
Siège social – Store/Magasin :
61, rue Sparks Street,
Ottawa, Ontario K1P 5A6
Tel. (613)238-8985. 1-800-267-4164
Store/Magasin : 211, rue Yonge Street,
Toronto, Ontario M5B 1M4.
Tel. (416)363-3171
Regional Sales Office/
Bureau des Ventes régional :
7575 Trans-Canada Hwy., Suite 305,
Saint-Laurent, Quebec H4T 1V6
Tel. (514)335-9274

DENMARK - DANEMARK
Munksgaard Export and Subscription Service
35, Nørre Søgade, DK-1370 København K
Tel. +45.1.12.85.70

FINLAND - FINLANDE
Akateeminen Kirjakauppa,
Keskuskatu 1, 00100 Helsinki 10   Tel. 0.12141

FRANCE
OCDE/OECD
Mail Orders/Commandes par correspondance :
2, rue André-Pascal,
75775 Paris Cedex 16
Tel. (1) 45.24.82.00
Bookshop/Librairie : 33, rue Octave-Feuillet
75016 Paris
Tel. (1) 45.24.81.67 et/ou (1) 45.24.81.81
Principal correspondant :
Librairie de l'Université,
12a, rue Nazareth,
13602 Aix-en-Provence   Tel. 42.26.18.08

GERMANY - ALLEMAGNE
OECD Publications and Information Centre,
4 Simrockstrasse,
5300 Bonn   Tel. (0228) 21.60.45

GREECE - GRÈCE
Librairie Kauffmann,
28, rue du Stade, 105 64 Athens   Tel. 322.21.60

HONG KONG
Government Information Services,
Publications (Sales) Office,
Beaconsfield House, 4/F.,
Queen's Road Central

ICELAND - ISLANDE
Snæbjörn Jónsson & Co., h.f.,
Hafnarstræti 4 & 9,
P.O.B. 1131 – Reykjavik
Tel. 13133/14281/11936

INDIA - INDE
Oxford Book and Stationery Co.,
Scindia House, New Delhi 1   Tel. 45896
17 Park St., Calcutta 700016   Tel. 240832

INDONESIA - INDONESIE
Pdin Lipi, P.O. Box 3065/JKT.Jakarta
Tel. 583467

IRELAND - IRLANDE
TDC Publishers – Library Suppliers
12 North Frederick Street, Dublin 1
Tel. 744835-749677

ITALY - ITALIE
Libreria Commissionaria Sansoni,
Via Lamarmora 45, 50121 Firenze
Tel. 579751/584468
Via Bartolini 29, 20155 Milano   Tel. 365083
Sub-depositari :
Ugo Tassi, Via A. Farnese 28,
00192 Roma   Tel. 310590
Editrice e Libreria Herder,
Piazza Montecitorio 120, 00186 Roma
Tel. 6794628
Agenzia Libraria Pegaso,
Via de Romita 5, 70121 Bari
Tel. 540.105/540.195
Agenzia Libraria Pegaso, Via S.Anna dei
Lombardi 16, 80134 Napoli.   Tel. 314180
Libreria Hœpli,
Via Hœpli 5, 20121 Milano   Tel. 865446
Libreria Scientifica
Dott. Lucio de Biasio "Aeiou"
Via Meravigli 16, 20123 Milano   Tel. 807679
Libreria Zanichelli, Piazza Galvani 1/A,
40124 Bologna   Tel. 237389
Libreria Lattes,
Via Garibaldi 3, 10122 Torino   Tel. 519274
La diffusione delle edizioni OCSE è inoltre
assicurata dalle migliori librerie nelle città più
importanti.

JAPAN - JAPON
OECD Publications and Information Centre,
Landic Akasaka Bldg., 2-3-4 Akasaka,
Minato-ku, Tokyo 107   Tel. 586.2016

KOREA - CORÉE
Pan Korea Book Corporation
P.O.Box No. 101 Kwangwhamun, Seoul
Tel. 72.7369

LEBANON - LIBAN
Documenta Scientifica/Redico,
Edison Building, Bliss St.,
P.O.B. 5641, Beirut   Tel. 354429-344425

MALAYSIA - MALAISIE
University of Malaya Co-operative Bookshop
Ltd.,
P.O.Box 1127, Jalan Pantai Baru,
Kuala Lumpur   Tel. 577701/577072

NETHERLANDS - PAYS-BAS
Staatsuitgeverij Verzendboekhandel
Chr. Plantijnstraat, 1 Postbus 20014
2500 EA S-Gravenhage   Tel. 070-789911
Voor bestellingen: Tel. 070-789208

NEW ZEALAND - NOUVELLE-ZÉLANDE
Government Printing Office Bookshops:
Auckland: Retail Bookshop, 25 Rutland Street,
Mail Orders, 85 Beach Road
Private Bag C.P.O.
Hamilton: Retail: Ward Street,
Mail Orders, P.O. Box 857
Wellington: Retail, Mulgrave Street, (Head
Office)
Cubacade World Trade Centre,
Mail Orders, Private Bag
Christchurch: Retail, 159 Hereford Street,
Mail Orders, Private Bag
Dunedin: Retail, Princes Street,
Mail Orders, P.O. Box 1104

NORWAY - NORVÈGE
Tanum-Karl Johan a.s
P.O. Box 1177 Sentrum, 0107 Oslo 1
Tel. (02) 801260

PAKISTAN
Mirza Book Agency
65 Shahrah Quaid-E-Azam, Lahore 3 Tel. 66839

PORTUGAL
Livraria Portugal,
Rua do Carmo 70-74, 1117 Lisboa Codex.
Tel. 360582/3

SINGAPORE - SINGAPOUR
Information Publications Pte Ltd
Pei-Fu Industrial Building,
24 New Industrial Road No. 02-06
Singapore 1953   Tel. 2831786, 2831798

SPAIN - ESPAGNE
Mundi-Prensa Libros, S.A.,
Castelló 37, Apartado 1223, Madrid-28001
Tel. 431.33.99
Libreria Bosch, Ronda Universidad 11,
Barcelona 7   Tel. 317.53.08/317.53.58

SWEDEN - SUÈDE
AB CE Fritzes Kungl. Hovbokhandel,
Box 16356, S 103 27 STH,
Regeringsgatan 12,
DS Stockholm   Tel. (08) 23.89.00
Subscription Agency/Abonnements:
Wennergren-Williams AB,
Box 30004, S104 25 Stockholm. Tel. 08/54.12.00

SWITZERLAND - SUISSE
OECD Publications and Information Centre,
4 Simrockstrasse,
5300 Bonn (Germany)   Tel. (0228) 21.60.45
Local Agent:
Librairie Payot,
6 rue Grenus, 1211 Genève 11
Tel. (022) 31.89.50

TAIWAN - FORMOSE
Good Faith Worldwide Int'l Co., Ltd.
9th floor, No. 118, Sec.2
Chung Hsiao E. Road
Taipei   Tel. 391.7396/391.7397

THAILAND - THAILANDE
Suksit Siam Co., Ltd.,
1715 Rama IV Rd.,
Samyam Bangkok 5   Tel. 2511630

TURKEY - TURQUIE
Kültur Yayinlari Is-Türk Ltd. Sti.
Atatürk Bulvari No: 191/Kat. 21
Kavaklidere/Ankara   Tel. 17.02.66
Dolmabahce Cad. No: 29
Besiktas/Istanbul   Tel. 60.71.88

UNITED KINGDOM - ROYAUME UNI
H.M. Stationery Office,
Postal orders only:
P.O.B. 276, London SW8 5DT
Telephone orders: (01) 622.3316, or
Personal callers:
49 High Holborn, London WC1V 6HB
Branches at: Belfast, Birmingham,
Bristol, Edinburgh, Manchester

UNITED STATES - ÉTATS-UNIS
OECD Publications and Information Centre,
Suite 1207, 1750 Pennsylvania Ave., N.W.,
Washington, D.C. 20006 - 4582
Tel. (202) 724.1857

VENEZUELA
Libreria del Este,
Avda F. Miranda 52, Aptdo. 60337,
Edificio Galipan, Caracas 106
Tel. 32.23.01/33.26.04/31.58.38

YUGOSLAVIA - YOUGOSLAVIE
Jugoslovenska Knjiga, Knez Mihajlova 2,
P.O.B. 36, Beograd   Tel. 621.992

Orders and inquiries from countries where Sales
Agents have not yet been appointed should be sent
to:
OECD, Publications Service, Sales and
Distribution Division, 2, rue André-Pascal, 75775
PARIS CEDEX 16.

Les commandes provenant de pays où l'OCDE n'a
pas encore désigné de dépositaire peuvent être
adressées à :
OCDE, Service des Publications. Division des
Ventes et-Distribution. 2. rue André-Pascal. 75775
PARIS CEDEX 16.

69777-06-1986

OECD PUBLICATIONS
2, rue André-Pascal
75775 PARIS CEDEX 16
No. 43685
(10 86 31 1) ISBN 92-64-12841-7
ISSN 0376-6438

•

PRINTED IN FRANCE